INITIATION

AND ITS

RESULTS

A Sequel to
"THE WAY OF INITIATION"
(1909)

Contents: The Astral Centers (Chakras); The Constitution of the Etheric Body; Dream-Life; The Three States of Consciousness; The Disassociation of the Human Personality During Initiation; The First Guardian of the Threshold; The Second Guardian of the Threshold—Life and Death.

CHALICE.

Rudolph Steiner

ISBN 1-56459-607-9

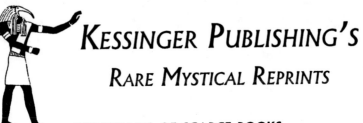

FOREWORD

THE widespread interest taken in the first volume of this series (entitled "THE WAY OF INITIATION"), and its success, have encouraged me to place before English readers, in the present volume, a translation of the articles written by Dr. Steiner as a sequel to the above series, and originally published in *Lucifer Gnosis* (Nos. 20-28), a theosophical magazine, published by M. Altmann, Leipzig, and edited by Dr. Rudolf Steiner. The same magazine is now bringing out a series of articles, entitled "The Theory of Cognition according to Occultism," which, when finished, will conclude these very important communications from a source of genuine occult wisdom. When completed, I propose to publish them as a third volume of this series.

To save disappointment to some readers into whose hands this book may chance to fall, let me frankly state at the outset that neither this nor its companion volumes are intended for people who deny the possibility of attaining knowledge by other means than their physical organs of sense ; the belief in, or at least the hypothetical acceptance of the reality of the unseen world and of forces not perceptible by our physical senses is therein taken for granted. For those unable to accept these premises there exists a vast literature which, if approached with an unprejudiced mind and carefully studied, will convince them of all that is here postulated.

These volumes might be called *advanced* text-books of occultism, and those to whom the subject is repellent had better not read them, because they are written by an occultist of a very high order for those really interested in the subject, and desirous of advancing in their self-development to a point hitherto unattainable by them, since it has not until now been deemed expedient openly to publish such far-reaching revelations of the occult. The book is intended for those only who will use every power gained for the helping of their fellow-pilgrims, and who place self-sacrifice and unselfish devotion to the best interests of mankind above all other virtues.

On the other hand, there is a large number of people, deeply interested in the subject, who were under the impression that there is only the one occultism whose home is in the East, and who now eagerly welcome a teaching, sprung from a *Western* source, which shows them that they need not go beyond Europe in their search either for genuine occult knowledge, or for teachers competent to instruct those willing to fulfil the conditions necessary for the safe treading of the narrow Path leading up to the feet of the One Initiator.

There are few leaders of thought at the present day who have a larger following than Dr. Steiner in the German-speaking part of Mid-Europe, and I know of no other teacher able to gather around him from 400 to 500 cultured people who will eagerly travel any distance and stay for two or three weeks wherever he may choose to lecture. During his recent courses of addresses on the Apocalypse, the Gospel according to St. John, " From Buddha to Christ," on Cosmogony, etc. etc., held in Berlin and Bâle, in Christiania and Budapest, in Munich and Rome—to mention only a few of the cities visited by this indefatigable worker for the good of humanity,—students were gathered together from all parts of Europe; from Hammerfest in the North and Palermo in the South, from Eastern Siberia, and from France and Spain.

That we are living at present in a wonderful time of transition, when

"The old order changeth, yielding place to new,"

may be gathered from the fact that a very large number of those most eager to welcome these wonderful teachings are recruited from highly cultured classes, whose predecessors of but two decades ago would have scoffed at the whole subject.

In conclusion, I should like to draw attention to the close and wonderful relation which the careful student may trace between the exercises and "trials" set forth in "THE WAY OF INITIATION" and the means of vivification of the astral organs (chakras) described in this volume. After the success of the first volume, we are satisfied that there is a widespread demand

in English-speaking countries for the teachings of Theosophy as enunciated by Dr.
Steiner, and we shall try gradually to make
accessible to English readers all the more
important works of this truly great Mystic
and Occultist.

For those who are fully satisfied with
the exoteric teachings of the day this
volume is not intended, but it is earnestly
hoped that it may bring Light and Peace
to serious seekers after truth.

MAX GYSI.

BELSIZE LODGE, BELSIZE LANE,
LONDON, N.W.,
31st *August* 1909.

CONTENTS

I

THE ASTRAL CENTRES
(CHAKRAS)

IT is one of the essential principles of genuine occultism that he who devotes himself to a study of it should only do so with a complete understanding ; should neither undertake nor practise anything of which he does not realise the results. An occult teacher giving a person either instruction or counsel will invariably begin with an explanation of those changes in body, in soul, and in spirit, which will occur to him who seeks for the higher knowledge.

We shall consider here some of these

effects upon the soul of the occult student, for only he who is cognisant of what is now to be said can undertake with a full understanding the practices which will lead to a knowledge of the superphysical worlds. Indeed, one may say that it is only such who are genuine occult students. By true occultism all experimenting in the dark is very strongly discouraged. He who will not undergo with open eyes the period of schooling, may become a medium, but all such efforts cannot bring him to clairvoyance as it is understood by the occultist.

To those who, in the right way, have practised the methods (concerning the acquisition of superphysical knowledge) which were indicated in my book, entitled *The Way of Initiation*,[1] certain changes

[1] *The Way of Initiation, or How to Attain Knowledge of the Higher Worlds.* By Rudolf Steiner, Ph.D. With a foreword by Annie Besant, and some Biographical

occur in what is called " the astral body "
(the organism of the soul).   This organism
is only perceptible to the clairvoyant. *" see" things*
One may compare it to a more or less
luminous cloud which is discerned in the
midst of the physical body, and in this
astral body the impulses, desires, passions,
and ideas become visible.   Sensual
appetites, for example, are manifested
as dark-red outpourings of a particular
shape; a pure and noble thought is
expressed in an outpouring of reddish-
violet colour; the clear-cut conception of
a logical thinker will appear as a yellow
figure with quite sharp outlines; while the
confused thought of a cloudy brain is
manifested as a figure with vague outlines.   The thoughts of people with views
that are one-sided and firmly fixed will

Notes of the Author by Edouard Schuré.   Second
impression. 237 pp. Cloth. Crown 8vo. 3s. 6d. net.
Postage 4d. extra.

appear sharp in their outlines, but im-
mobile; while those of people who remain
accessible to other points of view are seen
to be in motion, with varying outlines.

The further the student now advances
in his psychic development, the more will
his astral body become regularly organised;
in the case of a person whose psychic life
is undeveloped, it remains ill-organised
and confused. Yet in such an unorganised
astral body the clairvoyant can perceive
a form which stands out clearly from its
environment. It extends from the interior
of the head to the middle of the physical
body. It appears as, in a certain sense,
an independent body possessed of special
organs. These organs, which are now to
be considered, are seen to exist in the
following parts of the physical body: the
first between the eyes; the second at the
larynx; the third in the region of the heart;
the fourth in what is called the pit of the

stomach; while the fifth and sixth are situated in the abdomen. Such forms are technically known as "wheels" (chakras) or "lotus-flowers." They are so called on account of their likeness to wheels or flowers, but of course it should be clearly understood that such an expression is not to be applied more literally than when one calls the lobes of the lungs the "wings." Just as everybody knows that here one is not really dealing with "wings," so must it be remembered that in respect of the "wheels" one is merely speaking figuratively. These "lotus-flowers" are at present, in the undeveloped person, of dark colours and without movement—inert. In the clairvoyant, however, they are seen to be in motion and of luminous colour. In the medium something similar happens, albeit in a different way; but that part of the subject cannot now be pursued any further. As soon as the occult student begins his practices, the lotus-flowers first become lucent; later on they begin to revolve. It is when this occurs that the faculty of clairvoyance begins. For these "flowers" are the sense-organs of the soul, and their revolutions make manifest the fact that one is able to perceive in the superphysical world. No one can behold any superphysical thing until he has in this way developed his astral senses.

The sense-organ, which is situated in the vicinity of the larynx, allows one to perceive clairvoyantly the thoughts of another person, and also brings a deeper insight into the true laws of natural phenomena. The organ situated near the heart permits of a clairvoyant knowledge concerning the sentiments of another person. He who has developed it can also observe certain of the deeper powers in animals and plants. By means of the

Throat = 16 petals

Throat chakra allows you to perceive clairvoyantly the thoughts of another person and true laws of natural phenomena.

Heart = 12 petals

Perceive the sentiments of another person. And deeper powers in animals and plants.

organ that lies in the pit of the stomach one acquires knowledge of the capacities and talents of a person : by this, too, one is enabled to see what parts in the household of nature are played by animals, plants, stones, metals, atmospheric phenomena, and so on.

The organ situated at the larynx has sixteen "petals" or "spokes"; that which is in the region of the heart has twelve; that which is in the pit of the stomach has ten. Now certain activities of the soul are connected with the development of these sense-organs, and he who practises them in a particular way contributes something to the development of the astral organs concerned. Eight of the sixteen petals of the "lotus" have been developed already during an earlier stage of human evolution, in a remote past. To this development the human being contributed nothing. He held them as

(10 petals)

Solar plexus = knowledge to the capacities and talents of a person. Also, can see in the household I have are played by animals, plants, stones, etc.

a gift of Nature, when he was yet in a dreamy, dull state of consciousness. At that stage of human evolution they were already active. The manner of their activity, however, was only compatible with the dull state of consciousness already mentioned. As consciousness then grew brighter, the petals became obscure and withdrew their activity. The other eight can be developed by a person's conscious practice, and after that the entire lotus becomes both brilliant and active. The acquisition of certain capacities depends upon the development of everyone of these petals. Yet, as already shown, one can only consciously develop eight of them; the other eight reappear spontaneously.

Their development is consummated in the following manner. One must apply oneself with care and attention to certain functions of the soul which one usually exercises in a careless manner and without attention. There are eight such functions. The first depends on the manner in which one receives ideas. People usually allow themselves to be led in this respect by chance alone. They hear this and that, they see one thing and another, upon which they base their ideas. While this is the case the sixteen petals of the lotus remain quite torpid. Only when one begins in this matter to take one's education into one's own hands do they really begin to be effective. All conceptions must be guarded with this end in view. Every idea should have some significance. One ought to see in it a certain message, a fragment of knowledge concerning the things of the outer world, and one must not be satisfied with conceptions that have no such significance. One should so govern one's mental life that it becomes a mirror of the outer world, and should direct one's energies to the expulsion of incorrect ideas.

The second of these functions is concerned, in a similar way, with the control of the resolutions. One should only make resolutions after a well-founded, full consideration of even the most insignificant points. All thoughtless deeds, all meaningless actions, should be put far away from the soul. For everything one must have well-considered grounds, and one ought never to do a thing for which there is no real need.

The third function relates to speech. The occult student should only utter what is sensible and purposeful. All talking for the sake of talking draws him away from his path. He must avoid the usual method of conversation, in which all manner of things, unselected and heterogeneous, are spoken of together. In accomplishing this, however, he must not preclude him-

1.) Thoughtless deeds, meaningless actions

2.) All thoughtless deeds s/b be meaningless actions s/b be put far away from the soul in which don't do anything for which there is no real need will everything must have considered grounds.

3.) Speech Only utter what is sensible and purposeful. conversation s/b not in similar and useful grown in manner of conversation proper usual manner

4.) Regulate outward actions. Regular actions disturbing to others. But Harmonises with environment.

self from intercourse with his fellows. Precisely in such intercourse ought his conversation to grow in significance. He answers everybody, but he does so thoughtfully and after careful consideration of the question. He never speaks without grounds for what he says. He seeks to use neither too many nor too few words.

The fourth function is the regulation of outward action. The student seeks to direct his actions in such a way that it fits in with the actions of his fellow-men and with the peculiarities of his environment. He rejects all actions that are disturbing to others or that are antagonistic to those which are customary around him. He tries so to act that his deeds may combine harmoniously with his environment, with his position in life, and so forth. Where he is caused to act by some external suggestion he considers carefully how he can best respond. Where he is his own master, he considers the effects of his methods of action with the utmost care.

The fifth activity here to be noticed lies in the management of the entire life. The occult student endeavours to live in conformity with both Nature and Spirit. Never over-hasty, he is also never idle. Indolence and superfluous activity lie equally far away from him. He looks upon life as a means for work and he lives accordingly. He arranges habits, and fosters health so that a harmonious life is the outcome.

The sixth is concerned with human endeavour. The student tests his capacities and his knowledge and conducts himself in the light of such self-knowledge. He tries to perform nothing that is beyond his powers; but also to omit nothing for which they inwardly seem adequate. On the other hand, he sets before himself aims that coincide with the ideal, with the high duty of a human being. He does not merely regard himself half thoughtlessly as a wheel in the vast machinery of mankind, but endeavours to comprehend its problems, to look out beyond the trivial and the daily. He thus endeavours to fulfil his obligations ever better and more perfectly.

The seventh change in the life of his soul deals with the effort to learn as much from life as possible. Nothing passes before the student without giving him occasion to accumulate experience which is of value to him for life. If he has done anything wrongly or imperfectly, it offers an opportunity later on to make it correspondingly either right or perfect. If he sees others act, he watches them with a similar intent. He tries to collect from experience a rich treasure, and ever to consult it attentively ; nor, indeed, will he do anything without having looked back over experiences that can give him help in his decisions and actions.

Finally, the eighth is this : the student must from time to time look inward, sink back into himself, take careful counsel with himself, build up and test the foundations of his life, run over his store of knowledge, ponder upon his duties, consider the contents and aim of life, and so forth. All these matters have already been mentioned in *The Way of Initiation* (see page 2); here they are merely recapitulated in connection with the development of the sixteen-petalled lotus. By means of these exercises it will become ever more and more perfect, for upon such practices depends the development of clairvoyance. For instance, the more what a person thinks and utters harmonises with the actual occurrences of the outer world, the more quickly will he develop this faculty. He who thinks or speaks anything that is untrue kills something in the bud of the sixteen-petalled lotus. Truthfulness, Uprightness, and Honesty are in this connection formative, but Falsehood, Simulation, and Dishonesty are destructive forces. The student must recognise that not merely " good intentions " are needed, but also actual deeds. If I think or say anything which does not harmonise with the truth, I kill something in my astral organs, even although I believed myself to speak or think from intentions ever so good. It is here as with the child who needs must burn itself if it falls into the fire, even although this may have occurred from ignorance. The regulation of the above-mentioned activities of the soul in the manner described, allows the sixteen-petalled lotus to ray forth in splendid hues and imparts to it a definite movement. Yet it must be remarked that the signs of clairvoyant faculty cannot appear before a certain stage of this development is reached. So long as it is a trouble to lead this kind of life the faculty remains unmanifested. So long as one has to give special thought to the matters already described, one is yet unripe. Only when one has carried them so far that one lives quite habitually in the specified manner can the preliminary traces of clairvoyance appear. These matters must therefore no longer seem troublesome, but must become the habitual way of life. There is no need to watch oneself continually, nor to force oneself on to such a life. Everything must become habitual. There are certain instructions by the fulfilment of which the lotus may be brought to blossom in another way. But such methods are rejected by true occultism, for they lead to the destruction of physical health and to the ruin of morality. They are easier to accomplish than those described, which are protracted and troublesome, but the latter lead to the true goal and cannot but strengthen morality. (The student will notice that the spiritual practices described above correspond to what is called in Buddhism "the eightfold path." Here the connection between that path and the upbuilding of the astral organs must be explained.)

If to all that has been said there is added the observance of certain orders which the student may only receive orally from the teacher, there results an acceleration in the development of the sixteen-petalled lotus. But such instructions cannot be given outside the precincts of an occult school. Yet the regulation of life in the way described is also useful for those who will not, or cannot, attach themselves to a school. For the effect upon the astral body occurs in every case, even if it be but slowly. To the occult pupil the observance of these principles is indispensable. If he should try to train himself in occultism without observing them, he could only enter the higher world with defective mental eyes; and in place of knowing the truth he would then be merely subject to deception and illusion. In a certain direction he might become clairvoyant; but fundamentally nothing but a blindness completer than of old would beset him. For hitherto he stood at least firmly in the midst of the sense-world and had in it a certain support; but now he sees beyond that world and will fall into error concerning it before he is able to stand securely in a higher sphere. As a rule, indeed, he cannot distinguish error from truth, and he loses all direction in life. For this very reason is patience in such matters essential. It must always be remembered that the occult teacher may not proceed very far with his instructions unless an earnest desire for a regulated development of the lotus - flowers is already present. Only mere caricatures of these flowers could be evolved if they were brought to blossom before they had acquired, in a steady manner, their appropriate form. For the special instructions of the teacher bring about the blossoming of the lotuses, but form is imparted to them by the manner of life already outlined.

The irregular development of a lotus-flower has, for its result, not only illusion and fantastic conceptions where a certain kind of clairvoyance has occurred, but also errors and lack of balance in life itself. Through such development one may well become timid, envious, conceited, self-willed, stiff-necked, and so on, while hitherto one may have possessed none of these characteristics. It has already been said that eight petals of the lotus were developed long ago, in a very remote past, and that these in the course of occult education unfold again of themselves. In the instruction of the student, all care must now be given to the other eight. By erroneous teaching the former may easily appear alone, and the latter remain untended and inert. This would be the case particularly when too little logical, reasonable thinking is introduced into the instruction. It is of supreme importance that the student should be a sensible and clear-thinking person, and of equal importance that he should practise the greatest clarity of speech. People who begin to have some presentiment of superphysical things are apt to become talkative about such things. In that way they retard their development. The less one talks about these matters the better. Only he who has come to a certain stage of clearness ought to speak of them.

At the commencement of the instruc-

tions occult students are astonished, as
a rule, to find how little curiosity the
teacher exhibits concerning their experiences. It were best of all for them if they
were to remain entirely uncommunicative
about these experiences, and should say
nothing further than how successful or how
unsuccessful they had been in the perform-
ance of their exercises or in the observance
of their instructions. The occult teacher
has quite other means of estimating their
progress than their own communications.
The eight petals now under consideration
always become a little hardened through
such communication where they ought
really to grow soft and supple. An illustration shall be given to explain this, not
taken from the superphysical world, but,
for the sake of clearness, from ordinary
life. Suppose that I hear a piece of
news and thereupon form at once an
opinion. In a little while I receive

some further news which does not harmonise with the previous information.   I
am constrained thereby to reverse my
original judgment.   The result of this is an
unfavourable influence upon my sixteen-
petalled lotus.   It would have been quite
otherwise if, in the first place, I had sus-
pended my judgment; if concerning the
whole affair I had remained, inwardly in
thought and outwardly in words, entirely
silent until I had acquired quite reliable
grounds for the formation of my judgment.
Caution in the formation and the pro-
nouncement of opinions becomes, by
degrees, the special characteristic of the
occult student.   Thereby he increases
his sensibility to impressions and experiences, which he allows to pass over him
silently in order to collect the largest possible number of facts from which to form
his opinions.   There exist in the lotus-
flower bluish-red and rose-red shades of

colour which manifest themselves under the influence of such circumspection, while in the opposite case orange and dark red shades would appear.

The twelve-petalled lotus which lies in the region of the heart is formed in a similar way. Half its petals, likewise, were already existent and active in a remote stage of human evolution. These six petals do not require to be especially evolved in the occult school: they appear spontaneously and begin to revolve when we set to work on the other six. In the cultivation of these, as in the previous case, one has to control and direct certain activities of the mind in a special way.

It must be clearly understood that the perceptions of each astral or soul-organ bear a peculiar character. The twelve-petalled lotus possesses perception of quite a different kind from that of the sixteen petals. The latter perceives forms. The thoughts of a person and the laws under which a natural phenomenon takes place appear to the sixteen-petalled lotus as forms—not, however, rigid, motionless forms, but active and filled with life. The clairvoyant, in whom this sense is well evolved, can discern a form wherewith every thought, every natural law, finds expression. A thought of vengeance, for example, manifests as an arrowlike, pronged form, while a thought of goodwill frequently takes the shape of an opening flower. Clear-cut, meaningful thoughts are formed regularly and symmetrically, while hazy conceptions take on hazy outlines. By means of the twelve-petalled flower quite different perceptions are acquired. Approximately one can indicate the nature of these perceptions by likening them to the sense of cold and heat. A clairvoyant equipped with this faculty feels a mental warmth or chilliness raying out from the forms discerned by means of the sixteen-petalled flower. If a clairvoyant had evolved the sixteen-petalled lotus, but not the lotus of twelve petals, he would only observe a thought of goodwill as the shape already described, while another in whom both senses were developed would also discern that outraying of the thought which one can only call a mental warmth. It may be remarked in passing that in the occult school one sense is never evolved without the other, so that what has just been said should only be regarded as having been stated for the sake of clarity. By the cultivation of the twelve-petalled lotus the clairvoyant discovers in himself a deep comprehension of natural processes. Everything that is growing or evolving rays out warmth; everything that is decaying, perishing, or in ruins, will seem cold.

The development of this sense may be accelerated in the following manner. The first requirement is that the student should apply himself to the regulation of his thoughts. Just as the sixteen-petalled lotus achieves its evolution by means of earnest and significant thinking, so is the twelve-petalled flower cultivated by means of an inward control over the currents of thought. Errant thoughts which follow each other in no logical or reasonable sequence, but merely by pure chance, destroy the form of the lotus in question. The more one thought follows another, the more all disconnected thought is thrown aside, the more does this astral organ assume its appropriate form. If the student hears illogical thought expressed, he should silently set it straight within his own mind. He ought not, for the purpose of perfecting his own development, to withdraw himself uncharitably from what is perhaps an illogical mental environment. Neither should he allow himself to feel

1.) Regulation of thoughts; stop chatter. Should not feel compelled to correct the illogical. Thinking around going to withdraw

2.) Control your actions in a like manner

3.) cultivate perseverance Obstacles are given

4.) TOLERANCE all persons, all circumstances. No attempts to change impulsive.

5.) Impartiality favor others

6.) a measure of balance in emotions of mind

impelled to correct the illogical thinking around him. Rather should he quietly, in his own inner self, constrain this whirl-pool of thoughts to a logical and reasonable course. And above all things ought he to strive after this regulation in the region of his own thoughts.

A second requirement is that he should control his actions in a similar way. All instability or disharmony of action produces a withering effect upon the lotus-flower which is here in consideration. If the student has done anything he should manage the succeeding act so that it forms a logical sequence to the first, for he who acts differently from day to day will never evolve this faculty or sense.

. The third requirement is the cultivation of perseverance. The occult student never allows himself to be drawn by this or that influence aside from his goal so long as he continues to believe that it is the right one.

Obstacles are for him like challenges to overcome them and never afford reasons for loitering on the way.

The fourth requirement is tolerance as regards all persons and circumstances. The student should seek to avoid all superfluous criticism of imperfections and vices, and should rather endeavour to comprehend everything that comes under his notice. Even as the sun does not refuse its light to the evil and the vicious, so he, too, should not refuse them an intelligent sympathy. If the student meets with some trouble, he should not waste his force in criticism, but bow to necessity and seek how he may try to transmute the misfortune into good. He does not look at another's opinions from his own standpoint alone, but seeks to put himself into his companion's position.

The fifth requirement is impartiality in one's relation to the affairs of life. In this

connection we speak of "trust" and "faith."
The occult student goes out to every person and every creature with this faith, and
through it he acts. He never says to himself, when anything is told to him, "I do
not believe that, since it is opposed to
my present opinions." Far rather is
he ready at any moment to test and
rearrange his opinions and ideas. He
always remains impressionable to everything that confronts him. Likewise does
he trust in the efficiency of what he
undertakes. Timidity and scepticism are
banished from his being. If he has any
purpose in view, he has also faith in its
power. A hundred failures cannot rob
him of this confidence. It is indeed that
"faith which can move mountains."

The sixth requirement is the cultivation
of a certain equanimity. The student
strives to temper his moods, whether they
come laden with sorrow or with joy. He

must avoid the extremes of rising up to
the sky in rapture or sinking down to the
earth in despair, but should constantly
control his mind and keep it evenly
balanced.   Sorrow and peril, joy and
prosperity alike find him ready armed.

The reader of theosophical literature
will find the qualities here described,
under the name of the "six attributes"
which must be striven after by him who
would attain to initiation.   Here their
connection with the astral sense, which
is called the twelve-petalled lotus, is to
be explained.   The teacher can impart
specific instructions which cause the
lotus to blossom ; but here, as before, the
development of its symmetrical form
depends upon the attributes already mentioned.   He who gives little or no heed
to that development will only form this
organ into a caricature of its proper shape.
It is possible to cultivate a certain clair-

voyance of this nature by directing these attributes to their evil side instead of to the good. A person may be intolerant, faint-hearted, and contentious toward his environment; may, for instance, perceive the sentiments of other people and either run away from them or hate them. This can be so accentuated that on account of the mental coldness which rays out to him from opinions which are contrary to his own, he cannot bear to listen to them, or else behaves in an objectionable manner.

The mental culture which is important for the development of the ten-petalled lotus is of a peculiarly delicate kind, for here it is a question of learning to domin-ate, in a particular manner, the very sense-impressions themselves. It is of especial importance to the clairvoyant at the out-set, for only by this faculty can he avoid a source of countless illusions and mental mirages. Usually, a person is not at all clear as to what things have dominion over his memories and fancies. Let us take the following case. Someone travels on the railway, and busies himself with a thought. Suddenly his thoughts take quite another direction. He then recollects an experience which he had some years ago, and interweaves it with his immediate thought. But he did not notice that his eyes have been turned toward the window, and were caught by the glance of a person who bears a likeness to someone else who was intimately concerned with the recollected experience. He remains unconscious of what he has seen and is only conscious of the results, and he therefore believes that the whole affair arose spontaneously. How much in life occurs in such a way! We play over things in our lives which we have read or experienced without bringing the connection into our consciousness. Some one, for instance, cannot bear a particular colour, but he does not realise that this is due to the fact that the school-teacher of whom he was afraid, many years ago, used to wear a coat of that colour. Innumerable illusions are based upon such associations. Many things penetrate to the soul without becoming embodied in the consciousness. The following case is a possible example. Some one reads in the paper about the death of a well-known person, and straightway is convinced that yesterday he had a presentiment about it, although he neither saw nor heard of anything that could have given rise to such a thought. It is quite true, the thought that this particular person would die, emerged yesterday "by itself," only he has failed to notice one thing. Two or three hours before this thought occurred to him yesterday he went to visit an acquaintance. A newspaper lay on the

3

table, but he did not read it.   Yet unconsciously his eyes fell upon an account of the dangerous illness in which the person concerned was lying.   He was not conscious of the impression, but the effects of it were, in reality, the whole substance of the "presentiment."

If one reflects upon such matters, one can measure how deep a source of illusion and fantasy they supply.   It is this that he who desires to foster the ten-petalled lotus must dam up, for by means of the latter one can perceive characteristics deeply embedded in human and other beings.   But the truth can only be extracted from these perceptions if one has entirely freed oneself from the delusions here described.   For this purpose it is necessary that one should become master of that which is carried in to one from the external world.   One must extend this mastery so far that veritably one does not receive those influences which one does not desire to receive, and this can only be achieved gradually by living a very powerful inward life. This must be so thoroughly done that one only allows those things to impress one on which one voluntarily directs the attention, and that one really prevents those impressions which might otherwise be unconsciously registered. What is seen must be voluntarily seen, and that to which no attention is given must actually no longer exist for oneself. The more vitally and energetically the soul does its inward work, the more will it acquire this power. The occult student must avoid all vague wanderings of sight or hearing. For him only those things to which he turns his eye or his ear must exist. He must practise the power of hearing nothing even in the loudest disturbance when he wishes to hear nothing: he must render his eyes unimpressionable to things which he does not especially desire to notice. He must be shielded as by a mental armour from all unconscious impressions. But in the region of his thoughts particularly must he apply himself in this respect. He puts a thought before him and only seeks to think such thoughts as, in full consciousness and freedom, he can relate to it. Fancy he rejects. If he finds himself anxious to connect one thought with another, he feels round carefully to discover how this latter thought occurred to him. He goes yet further. If, for instance, he has a particular antipathy for anything, he will wrestle with it and endeavour to find out some conscious connection between the antipathy and its object. In this way the unconscious elements in his soul become ever fewer and fewer. Only by such severe self-searching can the ten-petalled lotus attain the form which it ought to possess. The mental life of the occult student must be an attentive life, and he must know how to ignore completely everything which he does not wish, or ought not, to observe.

If such introspection is followed by a meditation, which is prescribed by the instructions of the teacher, the lotus-flower in the region of the pit of the stomach blossoms in the correct way, and that which had appeared (to the astral senses already described) as form and heat acquires also the characteristics of light and colour. Through this are revealed, for instance, the talents and capacities of people, the powers and the hidden attributes of Nature. The coloured aura of the living creature then becomes visible; all that is around us then manifests its spiritual attributes. It will be obvious that the very greatest care is necessary in the development of this province, for

the play of unconscious memories is here
exceedingly active. If this were not the
case, many people would possess the sense
now under consideration, for it appears
almost immediately if a person has really
got the impressions of his senses so completely under his power that they depend
on nothing but his attention or inattention.
Only so long as the dominion of the senses
holds the soul in subjection and dullness,
does it remain inactive.

Of greater difficulty than the development of this lotus is that of the six-petalled
flower which is situated in the centre
of the body. For to cultivate this it
is necessary to strive after a complete
mastery of the whole personality by means
of self-consciousness, so that body, soul,
and spirit make but one harmony. The
functions of the body, the inclinations and
passions of the soul, the thoughts and ideas
of the spirit must be brought into com-

plete union with each other. The body must be so refined and purified that its organs assimilate nothing which may not be of service to the soul and spirit. The soul must assimilate nothing through the body, whether of passion or desire, which is antagonistic to pure and noble thoughts. The spirit must not dominate the soul with laws and obligations like a slave-owner, but rather must the soul learn to follow by inclination and free choice these laws and duties. The duties of an occult student must not rule him as by a power to which he unwillingly submits, but rather as by something which he fulfils because he likes it. He must evolve a free soul which has attained an equilibrium between sense and spirit. He must carry this so far that he can abandon himself to the sense because it has been so ennobled that it has lost the power to drag him down. He must no longer require to curb his passions, inasmuch as they follow the good by themselves. As long as a person has to chastise himself he cannot arrive at a certain stage of occult education, for a virtue to which one has to constrain oneself is then valueless. As long as one retains a desire, even although one struggles not to comply therewith, it upsets one's development, nor does it matter whether this appetite be of the soul or of the body. For example, if some one avoids a particular stimulant for the purpose of purifying himself by refining his pleasures, it can only benefit him if his body suffers nothing by this deprivation. If this be not the case it is an indication that the body requires the stimulant, and the renunciation is then worthless. In this case it may even be true that the person in question must first of all forego the desirable goal and wait until favourable conditions—perhaps only in another life—

shall surround him.   A tempered renunciation is, under certain circumstances, a
much greater acquisition than the struggle
for something which in given conditions
remains unattainable.   Indeed, such a
tempered renunciation contributes more
than such struggle to one's development.

He who has evolved the six-petalled
lotus can communicate with beings who
are native to the higher worlds, though
even then only if their presence is manifested in the astral or soul-world.   In an
occult school, however, no instructions
concerning the development of this lotus-
flower would be imparted before the
student had trodden far enough on the
upward path to permit of his spirit
mounting into a yet higher world.   The
formation of these lotus-flowers must
always be accompanied by entrance into
this really spiritual sphere.   Otherwise
the student would fall into error and

uncertainty. He would undoubtedly be able to see, but he would remain incapable of estimating rightly the phenomena there seen. Now there already exists in him who has learned to evolve the six-petalled lotus, a security from error and giddiness, for no one who has acquired complete equilibrium of sense (or body), passion (or soul), and thought (or spirit) will be easily led into mistakes. Nothing is more essential than this security when, by the development of the six-petalled lotus, beings possessed of life and independence, and belonging to a world so completely hidden from his physical senses, are revealed before the spirit of the student. In order to ensure the necessary safety in this world, it is not enough to have cultivated the lotus-flowers, since he must have yet higher organs at his disposal.

II

THE CONSTITUTION OF THE ETHERIC BODY

THE cultivation of the astral body, as it has been described in the foregoing chapter, permits of a person perceiving supersensual phenomena, but he who would really find his way about the astral world must not tarry at this stage of evolution. The mere motion of the lotus-flowers does not really suffice. The student should be able to regulate and control the movement of his astral organs independently, and with complete consciousness. Otherwise, he would become, as it were, a plaything for external forces

43

and powers. If he does not wish to become such, he must acquire the faculty of hearing what is known as "the inner word," and to effect this it is needful to evolve not merely the astral but also the etheric body. This is the fine body which to the eyes of the clairvoyant appears as a kind of wraith of the physical body. It is to some extent a medium between the physical and the astral bodies. If one is equipped with clairvoyant powers, one can quite consciously suggest away the physical body of a person. On that higher plane it is no more than what is ordinarily an exercise of one's attention. Just as a person can withdraw his attention from anything that is before him so that it does not exist for him, so can the clairvoyant blot out a physical body from his observation so that it becomes, for him, physically transparent. If he applies this power to a human being who stands in front of him, nothing remains in his soul-sight except the etheric body and the astral body, which is greater than either of the other two and interpenetrates them both. The etheric body has approximately the size and form of the physical body, so that it practically fills the same space. It is an extremely delicate and finely-organised vehicle.[1] Its principal colour is different from the seven contained in the rainbow. He who is able to observe it is introduced to a colour which is not observable by the sense-perceptions. It can be compared to the colour of a young peach-blossom as accurately as to any. If one desires to contemplate the etheric body alone, one has to extinguish one's

[1] I would request the physicist not to resent the expression "etheric body." The use of the word "ether" is merely an attempt to suggest the fineness of the phenomenon under consideration. It has practically no connection at all with the hypothetical ether of the physicist.

observation of the astral body by an exercise of attention similar to that already suggested. If one omits to do so, one's view of the etheric body is confused by the complete interpenetration of the astral body.

Now the particles of this etheric body are in continual motion. Countless currents pass through it in every direction. By these currents life itself is supported and regulated. Every body that has life, including the animals and plants, possesses such an etheric double. Even in minerals there are traces of it perceptible to the attentive observer. These currents and movements are almost entirely independent of the human will and consciousness, just as the action of the heart or stomach in the physical body is independent of our will. As long as a person does not take his development (in the sense of acquiring supersensual faculties) into his own hands, this independence remains. For his development at a certain stage consists precisely in adding to the unconscious independent outrayings and movements of the etheric body that by which the individual is enabled to influence them in a conscious manner by himself.

When his occult education has progressed so far that the lotus-flowers described in the foregoing chapters begin to bestir themselves, then the student is given certain directions which lead to the evocation of particular currents and movements within his etheric body. The object of these directions is to fashion in the region of the physical heart a kind of centre from which these outrayings and movements, with their manifold forms and colours, may go forth. The centre is, in reality, not merely a given point, but a most complicated structure, a really wonderful organ. It glows and shimmers with all kinds of colour and displays forms of the greatest symmetry—forms which are capable of transformation with astonishing speed. Other forms and outrayings of colour proceed from this organ to the other parts of the body, as also to those of the astral body, which they entirely pervade and illumine. The most important of these rays move, however, toward the lotus-flowers. They pervade each petal and regulate its revolutions ; then, streaming out at the points of the petals, they lose themselves in the surrounding space. The more evolved a person may be, the greater becomes the circumference to which these rays extend.

The twelve-petalled lotus-flower has a peculiarly close connection with the centre already described. The rays move directly into it, and from it proceed, on the one side, toward the sixteen-petalled and the two-petalled lotuses, and, on the other, the lower, side to the lotuses of eight, of six, and of four petals. This is the reason why the very greatest care must be given to the development of the twelve-petalled lotus. If any imperfection be there allowed, the entire formation of the whole structure must remain disorderly. From what has here been said, one may imagine how delicate and intimate is this occult education, and how strictly one has to conduct oneself if everything is to be developed in the proper way. It will now be quite evident that instruction concerning the development of supersensual faculties can only be given by one who has already experienced everything which he desires to awaken in another, and who is unquestionably in a position to know whether his instructions will be rewarded with success.

If the student follows out what is

4

prescribed for him in these instructions, he introduces into his etheric body outrayings and vibrations which are in harmony with the laws and the evolution of the world to which he belongs.   Consequently, these instructions are reflections of the great laws which govern the development of the world.   They consist of special exercises in meditation and in concentration, which, if appropriately practised, produce the results described.   The content of these instructions may only be imparted to the individual during his occult education. At certain periods these instructions must entirely pervade his soul with their content, so that he is inwardly, as it were, filled with it.   He starts quite simply with what is necessary above all things, a deepening and an interiorisation of the reasonable and sensible thought of the head.   This thought is thus made free and independent of all sense-impressions or experiences.

It is in a certain manner concentrated into a point which is entirely in the power of the individual. By doing this a preliminary centre for the rays of the etheric body is formed. This centre is not yet in the region of the heart, but in that of the head, and it appears to the clairvoyant as the outgoing point of the vibrations. Only that occult educational course is successful which creates this centre first. If this centre were from the outset transferred to the region of the heart, the clairvoyant could doubtless obtain glimpses of the higher worlds; but he would yet lack any true insight into the connection between these higher worlds and that of our senses, and this for the individual at a certain stage of the world's evolution is an unconditional necessity. The clairvoyant must not become a mere enthusiast; he must retain his footing upon firm earth.

The centre in the head, when it has

become duly settled, is then transferred
further down, that is to say, to the region
of the larynx.   This change is again
induced by a particular exercise of concentration.   Then the characteristic vibrations
of the etheric body stream forth from this
point, and illuminate the astral space that
surrounds the individual.

A further exercise enables the student
to determine for himself the position of
his etheric body.   Hitherto this position
depended upon the forces which came from
without or proceeded from the physical
body.   By means of such development
the individual is able to direct the etheric
body to all sides.   This faculty is effected
by outrayings which move approximately
along both hands and are centred in the
two-petalled lotus that is situated in the
region of the eyes.   As a result of all this,
the rays which flow forth from the larynx
are shaped into round forms of which a

quantity proceed to the two-petalled lotus, and from there take their way as undulating currents along the hands.

One finds as a further development that these currents branch out, ramify in a delicate manner, and become in a certain sense like wicker-work, so that the entire etheric body is enmeshed in a network. Since hitherto the etheric body has had no closure to externals, so that the life-currents of the great ocean of life flowed freely in and out, it now becomes necessary that impacts from outside should pass through this cuticle. Thus the individual becomes sensitive to these external streams : they become perceptible to him. The time has now come to give the complete system of rays and vibrations a centre in the heart. That, again, is accomplished by means of a meditative and concentrative exercise, and simultaneously the student attains the point at which he can hear the "inner word." All things now acquire for him a new significance. They become audible, as it were, in their innermost nature; they speak to him from their true being. The currents already described place him in touch with the interior of the world to which they appertain. He begins to mingle his life with the life of his environment, and can let it reverberate in the vibrations of his lotus-flowers. Thus the individual enters the spiritual world. If he has come so far, he acquires a new understanding of all that the great teachers of humanity have uttered. The sayings of the Buddha, for instance, now produce a new effect upon him. They pervade him with a beatitude of which he had never dreamed before. For the sound of the words now follows the movements and rhythms which he has formed within himself. He is now able to know directly how a person like the Buddha did not proclaim his own individual revelations, but those which flowed into him from the inmost being of all things. A fact must here be explained which could only be comprehended in the light of what has already been said. The many repetitions in the sayings of the Buddha are not rightly understood by the people of our present evolutionary stage. For the occult student they are like something upon which he may gladly let his inner senses rest, for they correspond to certain rhythmic movements in the etheric body. Devotional musing on these, with complete inward peace, creates a harmony with these movements, and because they themselves are echoes of certain universal rhythms which also at particular points repeat themselves and make regular returns to their former modes, the individual, listening to the wisdom of the

Buddha, puts himself into harmony with the secrets of the universe.

In the theosophical handbooks we meet with *four* attributes which must be developed by the student on what is called the probationary path, in order that he may attain the higher knowledge. The first is the faculty for discriminating between the eternal and the temporal, the true and the false, the truth and mere opinion. The second is a right estimate of the eternal and true as opposed to the perishable and illusory. The third faculty is that of practising the six qualities already mentioned in the foregoing chapters: thought-control, control of action, perseverance, tolerance, good faith, and equanimity. The fourth attribute necessary is the longing for freedom. A mere intellectual comprehension of what is included in these attributes is utterly worthless. They must become so incor-

porated into the soul that they endure
as inner habits. Let us take, for instance,
the first of these attributes—the discrimination between the eternal and the
temporal. One must so educate oneself
that quite naturally one discriminates
in everything that confronts one between
its impermanent characteristics and those
that will endure. This can only be
accomplished if in one's observation of
the external world one continues again
and again to make this attempt. At last
the gaze in quite a natural way discerns
what endures, just as hitherto it had satisfied itself with the impermanent. "All
that is impermanent is only a parable"—
that is a truth which becomes an obvious
conviction for the soul. And so, too, must
it be with the others of the four attributes
on the path of probation.

Now under the influence of these four
spiritual habits the etheric body actually

transforms itself. By the first—the discrimination between the true and the false—the centre already described is formed in the head and that in the larynx is prepared. The exercises of concentration, before mentioned, are above all things essential to any true formation. It is they that create, while the four spiritual habits bring to fruition. If the centre in the larynx has been prepared, the free control of the etheric body, as above explained, will follow, and its separation, its network covering, be produced by the correct estimating of the eternal as opposed to the impermanent. If the student acquires this power of estimation, the facts of the higher worlds will gradually become perceptible. Only it must not be thought that one has merely to perform those actions which appear to be important when measured by the intellect alone. The smallest action, every little thing accomplished, has something of importance in the vast household of the world, and it is only necessary that one should become conscious of this importance. It is not a question of underestimating the daily affairs of life, but of rightly estimating them. Enough has been said in the previous chapter of the six virtues of which the third attribute is composed. They are connected with the development of the twelve-petalled lotus in the region of the heart, and this, as already indicated, is associated with the life-current of the etheric body. The fourth attribute, which is the longing for freedom, serves to bring to fruition the etheric organ situated in the heart. If these attributes have become real spiritual habits, the individual frees himself from everything which only depends upon the capacities of his personal nature. He ceases to contemplate things from his

own separate standpoint. The limits of
his narrow self, which fetter him to this
outlook, disappear. The secrets of the
spiritual world reveal themselves to his
inner self. This is liberation. For all
fetters constrain the individual to regard
things and beings as if they corresponded
to his personal limitations. From this
personal manner of regarding things the
occult student must become independent
and free.

From this it will be clear that the
writings which have proceeded from the
mighty sages can become effective in the
innermost deeps of human nature. The
sayings concerning the four attributes
are just such emanations of "primeval
wisdom." They can be found under one
form or another in all the great religions.
The founders of the great religions did not
give mankind these teachings from vague
feeling. They based them on much firmer

foundations, because they were mighty Initiates. Out of their knowledge did they shape their moral teachings. They were aware how these would react upon the finer nature of men, and desired that the culture of these qualities should gradually lead to the organisation of that finer nature. To live according to these great religions is to work out one's own spiritual perfection, and only in so doing can one really serve the world. Self-perfection is in no wise selfish, for the imperfect man is also an imperfect servant of humanity and of the world. The more perfect one becomes the more does one serve the world. "If the rose adorns herself she adorns the garden."

The founders of religions are therefore the great magicians. That which comes from them flows into the souls of men and women, and thus with humanity the whole world moves forward. The founders of religions have consciously worked with this evolutionary process of humanity. One only understands the true meaning of religious instructions when one realises that they are the result of actual knowledge concerning the innermost depths of human nature.

The leaders of religion were mighty sages, and it is out of their knowledge that the ideals of humanity have sprung. Yet the individual comes nearer to these leaders when he uplifts himself in his own evolution to their heights.

If a person has evolved his etheric body in the manner just described, an entirely new life is opened up before him, and at the proper period in the course of his training he now receives that enlightenment which adapts him to this new existence. For example, he sees (by means of the sixteen-petalled lotus) the shapes of a higher world. He must then realise how different are these forms when caused by this or that object or being. In the first place, he should notice that he is able, in a certain manner, to influence some of these forms very powerfully by means of his thoughts and feelings, but others not at all, or only to a limited extent. One species of these figures will be altered immediately if the observer thinks to himself when they appear, " that is beautiful," and then in the course of his contemplation changes his thought and thinks " that is useful." It is particularly characteristic of the forms which come from minerals or from objects artistically made, that they possess the peculiarity of changing under every thought or feeling which is directed upon them by the observer. In a lesser degree this is also true of the forms that proceed from plants, and to a still smaller extent of those that are connected with animals. These forms are full of life and motion, but this motion only pertains to that part which is under the influence of human thought or feeling, and in the other parts it is effected by forces upon which a person can exercise no influence. Now there appears within this whole world a species of forms which are almost entirely unaffected by activities on the part of human beings. The student can convince himself that these forms proceed either from minerals or artificial shapes, and not from animals or plants. In order to make these things quite clear, he must now observe those forms which he can realise to have proceeded from the feelings, impulses, and passions of human beings. Yet he may find that upon these forms his own thoughts and feelings still hold some influence, even although it be comparatively small. There always remains a residuum of forms in this world upon which all such influences are less and less effective. Indeed, this residuum comprises a very large proportion of those forms which are usually discerned by the student at the outset of his career. He can only enlighten himself concerning the nature of this species by observing himself. He then learns that they were produced by himself, that what he does or wishes or wills finds expression in these forms. An impulse that dwells in him, a desire that he possesses, a purpose that he harbours, and so forth, are all manifested in these forms; indeed, his whole character displays itself in this world of shapes. By means of his thoughts and feelings a person can exercise an influence upon all the forms which do not come from himself; but upon those which are sent into the higher world from his own being he possesses no power when once he has created them.

Now it follows from what has been said

5

that from this higher aspect of human inner nature one's own world of impulses, desires, and conceptions is seen to express itself in outward shapes, just like all other beings or objects. To the higher knowledge the inner world appears as a part of the outer world. Just as anyone in the physical world who should be surrounded with mirrors could look at his physical form in that way, so, too, in a higher world does the spiritual self of man appear to him as an image reflected in a mirror.

At this stage of development the student has arrived at the point when he overcomes the "illusion of the personal self," as it has been expressed in theosophical books. He can now regard that inner personality as something external to himself, just as previously he recognised as external the things which affected his senses. Thus he learns by gradual experience to master himself as hitherto he mastered the beings around him.

If any one obtains a view into this higher world before his nature has been sufficiently prepared, he stands before the character-picture of his own soul as before an enigma. There his own impulses and passions confront him in the shapes of animals or, more seldom, of human beings. It is true that the animal forms of this world have never quite the appearance of those in the physical world, but still, they possess a remote resemblance. By the inexpert observer they may easily be taken for the same. When one enters this world, one must adopt an entirely new method of forming one's judgments. For, seeing that those things which properly pertain to the inner nature appear as external to oneself, they are only discerned as the mirrored reflections of what they really are. When, for instance, one perceives a number, one must reverse it as one would read what is seen in a mirror. 265 would mean in reality 562. One sees a sphere as if one were in the centre of it. One has therefore at first to translate correctly these inner perceptions. The attributes of the soul appear likewise as if in a mirror. A wish that is directed toward something outside appears as a form which moves toward the person who wished it. Passions that have their habitation in the lower part of human nature take on the forms of animals or of similar shapes that let themselves loose upon the individual. In reality these passions are struggling outward; it is in the external world that they seek for satisfaction, but this outward striving appears in the mirrored reflection as an attack upon the impassioned person.

If the student, before attaining the higher vision, has learned by quiet, sincere examination of himself to realise his own attributes, he will then, at the moment when his inner self appears to him as a mirrored reflection outside, find courage and power to conduct himself in the right way. People who have not practised such introspection sufficiently to enable them to know their own inner natures will not recognise themselves in these mirrored pictures and will mistake them for something foreign. Or they may become alarmed at the vision and say to themselves, because they cannot endure the sight, that the whole thing is nothing but an illusion which cannot lead them anywhere. In either case the person, by his unseasonable arrival at a certain stage in the development of his higher organisation, would stand disastrously in his own way.

It is absolutely necessary that the student should pass through this experi-

ence of spiritually seeing his own soul if
he is to press onward to higher things.
For in his own self he then possesses that
spirituality by which he can best judge.
If he has already acquired a fair realisation of his own personality in the physical
world, and when the picture of that personality first appears to him in the higher
world, he is then able to compare the one
with the other.   He can refer to the
higher as to a thing known to him, and in
this way can advance on firm ground.   If,
on the contrary, he were confronted by
numbers of other spiritual beings, he
would be able to gain hardly any information concerning their nature and attributes.
He would very soon feel the ground slip-
ping away from his feet.   It cannot too
often be repeated that a safe entrance into
the higher worlds can only follow a solid
knowledge and estimate of one's own
nature.

It is pictures, then, that the student meets on his way up to the higher worlds, for the realities which are expressed by these pictures are really in himself. He must soon become sufficiently mature to prevent himself from desiring, at this first stage, veritable realities, but to allow of his regarding these pictures as appropriate. But inwardly he soon learns something completely new from his observation of this picture-world. His lower self only exists for him as mirrored pictures, yet in the midst of these reflections appears the true reality that is his higher self. Out of the pictures of the lower personality the form of the spiritual ego becomes visible. Then from the latter threads are spun to other and higher spiritual realities.

This is the moment when the two-petalled lotus in the region of the eyes is required. If this now begins to stir, the individual attains the power of setting his higher ego in connection with spiritual, superhuman entities. The currents which flow from this lotus move so toward these higher entities that the movements here spoken of are fully apparent to the individual. Just as the light makes physical objects visible to the eyes, these currents reveal the spiritual things of the higher worlds. Through sinking himself into certain ideas which the teacher imparts to the pupil in personal intercourse, the latter learns to set in motion, and then to direct the currents proceeding from this lotus-flower of the eyes.

At this stage of development especially, what is meant by a really sound capacity for judgment and a clear, logical training is manifested. One has only to consider that here the higher self, which had hitherto slumbered unconscious and like a seed, is born into conscious existence.

One is here concerned not with a figurative, but with a veritable birth in the spiritual world, and the being now born, the higher self, if it is to be capable of life, must enter that world with all the necessary organs and conditions. Just as nature takes precautions that a child shall come into the world with well-formed ears and eyes, one must take precautions in the self-development of an individual, so that his higher self shall enter existence with the necessary attributes. These laws which have to do with the development of the higher organs of the spirit are no other than the sound, rational, and moral laws of the physical world. The spiritual ego matures in the physical self, as the child in the mother's womb. The health of the child depends upon the normal working of natural laws in the womb of the mother. The health of the spiritual self is similarly conditioned by

the laws of common intelligence and
reason that work in the physical life.   No
one who does not live and think healthily
in the physical world can give birth to a
sound spiritual self.   Natural and rational
life is the basis of all true spiritual evolution.   Just as the child, when still in the
womb of the mother, lives according to
natural forces which after its birth it uses
with its organs of sense, so the higher self
in a human being lives according to the
laws of the spiritual world even during
its physical incarceration; and even as
the child out of a vague sensational life
acquires the powers above mentioned, so
can a human being also acquire the
powers of the spiritual world before his
own higher self is born.   Indeed, he must
do this if the latter is to enter its world
as a completely developed being.   It
would be quite wrong for anyone to say,
" I cannot follow the teachings of the

mystic and theosophist until I can see them for myself," for if he should adopt this view, he could certainly never attain to genuine higher knowledge.

He would be in the same position as a child in the mother's womb who should reject the powers that would come to him through the mother, and should intend to wait until he could create them for himself. Even as the embryo of the child learns in its dim life to accept as right and good what is offered to it, so should it be with the person who is still blindfolded in relation to the truths declared in the teachings of mystic or theosophist. There is an insight, based upon intuition of the truth and a clear, sound, all-round critical reason, concerning these teachings, that exists before one can yet see spiritual things for oneself. First, one must learn the mystical wisdom, and by this very study prepare oneself to see. A person who should learn to see before he has prepared himself in this way would resemble a child who was born with eyes and ears but without a brain. The entire world of sound and colour would widen out before him, but he could make no use of it.

That which before appealed to the student through his sense of truth, his reason, and his intelligence, becomes, at the stage of occult education already described, his own experience. He now has a direct realisation of his higher self, and he learns how this higher self is connected with spiritual entities of a loftier nature and how it forms a union with them. He sees how the lower self descends from a higher world, and it is revealed to him how his higher nature outlasts the lower. Now he can distinguish between what is permanent in himself and what is perishable, and this is nothing less than the power to understand from his own observation the teachings concerning the incarnation of the higher self in the lower. It will now become plain to him that he stands in a lofty spiritual relation thereto, that his attributes and his destiny are originated by this very relation. He learns to know the law of his life, his Karma. He perceives that his lower self, as it at present shapes his destiny, is only one of the forms which can be adopted by his higher nature. He discerns the possibility stretching before his higher self, of working upon his own nature so that he may become ever more and more perfect. Now, too, he can penetrate into the great differences between human beings in regard to their comparative perfection. He will recognise that there are before him people who have already traversed the stages that still lie in front of him.

He discerns that the teachings and deeds of such people proceed from the inspiration of a higher world. All this he owes to his first glimpse into this higher world. Those who have been called "the masters of wisdom," "the great Initiates of humanity," will now begin to appear as veritable facts.

These are the treasures which the student at this stage owes to his development: insight into his higher self; into the doctrine of the incarnation of this higher self in a lower; into the laws by which life in the physical world is regulated according to its spiritual connections—in short, the law of Karma; and, finally, insight into the nature of the great Initiates.

Of the student who has arrived at this stage it is said that doubt has entirely vanished away. If he has already acquired a faith which is based upon reason and sound thought, there now appears in its place full knowledge and an insight which nothing whatsoever can make dim.

Religions have presented in their ceremonies, their sacraments, and their rites, external visible pictures of the higher spiritual beings and events. None but those who have not penetrated into the depths of the great religions can fail to notice this; but he who has seen for himself these spiritual realities will understand the great significance of each outward and visible act. Then for him the religious service itself becomes a representation of his own communion with the spiritual, superhuman world. One often finds it said in theosophical literature, even if not quite so plainly expressed, that the occult student at this stage becomes "free from superstition." Superstition in its essence is nothing but dependence upon outward and visible acts, without insight into the spiritual facts of which they are the expression.

It has been shown how the student, by arriving at this stage, becomes veritably a new person. Little by little he can now mature himself by means of the currents that come from the etheric body, until he can control the still higher vital element, that which is called " the fire of Kundalini," and by so doing can attain a completer liberty from the bondage of his physical body.

III

DREAM-LIFE

An intimation that the student has arrived at the stage of evolution described in the foregoing chapter is the change which comes over his dream-life. Hitherto his dreams were confused and haphazard, but now they begin to assume a more regular character. Their pictures begin to arrange themselves in an orderly way, like the phenomena of daily life. He can discern in them laws, causes, and effects. The contents of his dreams will likewise change. While hitherto he discerned only the reverberations of daily life, mixed impressions of his surroundings or of his physical condition, there now appear before him pictures of a world with which he had no acquaintance. At first, indeed, the general nature of his dreams will remain as of old in so far as the dream differentiates itself from waking phenomena by presenting in emblematical form whatever it wishes to express. This dramatisation cannot have escaped the notice of any attentive observer of dream-life. For instance, you may dream that you are catching some horrible creature and experiencing an unpleasant sensation in your hand. You wake up to discover that you are tightly holding a piece of the bed-clothes. The perception does not express itself plainly, but only through the allegorical image. Or you may dream that you are flying from some pursuer and in consequence you experience fear. On waking up you find that during sleep you had been suffering from palpitation of the heart. The stomach which is replete with indigestible food will cause uneasy dream-pictures. Occurrences in the neighbour-hood of the sleeping person may also reflect themselves allegorically in dreams. The striking of a clock may evoke the picture of soldiers marching by to the sound of their drums. Or a falling chair can become the origin of a complete dream-drama in which the sound of falling is translated into a gun report, and so forth. The more regulated dreams of the person whose etheric body has begun its development have also this allegorical method of expression, but they will cease to repeat merely the facts of the physical environment or of the sense-body. As these dreams which owe their origin to such things become orderly they are mixed up with similar dream-pictures which are the expression of things and events in another world. Here one has experiences that lie beyond the range of one's waking consciousness. Now it must never be fancied that any true mystic will then make the things which in this manner he experiences in dreams the basis of any authoritative account of the higher world. One must only consider such dream-experiences as hints of a higher development. Very soon, as a further result of this, we find that the pictures of the dreaming student are no longer, as hitherto, withdrawn by the guidance of a careful intellect, but are regulated thereby, and methodically considered like the conceptions and impressions of the waking consciousness. The difference between this dream-consciousness and the waking state grows ever smaller and smaller. The dreamer becomes, in the fullest meaning of the word, awake in his dream-life: that is to say, he can feel himself to be the master and leader of the pictures which then appear.

During his dreams the individual actually finds himself in a world which is other than that of his physical senses. But if he possesses only unevolved spiritual organs, he can receive from that world only the confused dramatisations already mentioned. It would only be as much at his disposal as would be the sense-world to a being equipped with nothing but the most rudimentary of eyes. In consequence he could only discern in this world the reflections and reverberations of ordinary life. Yet in dream he can see these, because his soul interweaves its daily perceptions as pictures into the stuff of which that other world consists. It must here be clearly understood that in addition to the workaday conscious life one leads in this world a second and unconscious existence. Everything that one perceives or thinks becomes impressed upon this other world.   Only if the lotus-flowers are evolved can one perceive these impressions. Now certain minute beginnings of the lotus-flowers are always at the disposal of anyone.   During daily consciousness he cannot perceive with them, because the impressions made on him are very faint. It is for similar reasons that during the daytime one cannot see the stars.   They cannot strike our perceptions when opposed by the fierce and active sunlight, and it is just in this way that faint spiritual impressions cannot make themselves felt in opposition to the masterful impressions of the physical senses.   When the door of outward sense is closed in sleep, these impressions can emerge confusedly, and then the dreamer remembers what he has experienced in another world.   Yet, as already remarked, at first these experiences are nothing more than that which conceptions related to the physical senses have impressed on the spiritual world. Only the developed lotus-flowers make it possible for manifestations which are unconnected with the physical world to show themselves. Out of the development of the etheric body arises a full knowledge concerning the impressions that are conveyed from one world to another. With this the student's communication with a new world has begun. He must now—by means of the instructions given in his occult training—first of all acquire a two-fold nature. It must become possible for him during waking hours to recall quite consciously the beings he has observed in dream. If he has acquired this faculty he will then become able to make these observations during his ordinary waking state. His attention will have become so concentrated upon spiritual impressions that these impressions need no longer vanish in the light of those which come through the senses, but are, as it were, always at hand.

If the student is able to do this, there then arises before his spiritual eyes something of the picture which has been described in a former chapter. He can now discern that what exists in the spiritual world is the origin of that which corresponds to it in the physical world, and, above all things, can he learn in this world to know his own higher self. The task that now confronts him is to grow, as it were, into this higher self, or, in other words, to regard it as his only true self, and also to conduct himself accordingly. He now retains, more and more, the conception and the vital realisation that his physical body and what hitherto he designated "himself" is only an instrument of the higher self. He takes an attitude toward his lower self, such as might be taken by some one limited to the world of sense with regard to some instrument or vehicle which serves him. Just as such a person would not consider the carriage in which he travelled to be himself, though he says " I travel," or " I go," so, too, the developed person, when he says "I go through the door," retains in his mind the conception, " I take my body through the door." This must become for him such an habitual idea that he never for a moment loses the firm ground of the physical world, that never a feeling of estrangement in the world of sense arises. If the student does not wish to become a mere fantastic or vain enthusiast, he must work with the higher consciousness, so that he does not impoverish his life in the physical world, but enriches it, even as the person who makes use of a railway instead of his own legs may enrich himself by going for a journey.

If the student has raised himself to such a life in the higher Ego, then—or still more probably during the acquisition of the higher consciousness—it will be revealed to him how he may stir into life what is called the fire of Kundalini which lies in the organ at the heart, and, further, how he may direct the currents described in a previous chapter.

This fire of Kundalini is an element of finer material which flows outward from this organ and streams in luminous loveliness through the self-moving lotus-flowers and the other canals of the evolved etheric body. Thence it radiates outward on the surrounding spiritual world and makes it spiritually visible, just as the sunshine falling upon the surrounding objects makes visible the physical world.

How this fire of Kundalini in the organ at the heart is fanned into life may only form the subject of actual occult training. Nothing can be said of it openly.

The spiritual world becomes plainly perceptible as composed of objects and beings only for the individual who in such a way can send the fire of Kundalini through his etheric body and into the outer world, so that its objects are illumined by it. From this it will be seen that a complete consciousness of an object in the spiritual world is entirely dependent upon the condition that the person himself has cast upon it the spiritual light. In reality the Ego, who has drawn forth this fire, no longer dwells in the physical human body at all, but (as has been already shown) apart from it. The organ at the heart is only the spot where the individual from without enkindles that fire. If he wished to do this, not here but elsewhere, then the spiritual perceptions produced by means of the fire would have no connection with the physical world. Yet one should relate all the higher spiritual things to the physical world itself, and through oneself should let them work in the latter. The organ at the heart is precisely the one through which the higher self makes use of the lower self as his instrument and whence the latter is directed.

The feeling which the developed person now bears toward the things of the spiritual world is quite other than that which is characteristic of ordinary people in relation to the physical world. The latter feel themselves to be in a certain part of the world of sense, and the objects they perceive are external to them. The spiritually evolved person feels himself to be united with the spiritual objects that he perceives, as if, indeed, he were within them. In spiritual space he veritably moves from place to place, and is therefore spoken of in the language of occult science as "the wanderer." He is practically without a home. Should he continue in this mere wandering, he would be unable to define clearly any object in spiritual space. Just as one defines an object or a locality in physical space by starting from a certain point, so must it also be in regard to the other world. He must seek for a place there which he practically completely explores,—a place of which he spiritually takes possession. This he must make his spiritual home and set everything in relation to it. The person who is living in the physical world sees everything in a like manner, as if he carried the ideas of his physical home wherever he went. Involuntarily a man from Berlin will describe London quite otherwise than a Parisian. Only there is a difference between the spiritual and the physical home.   Into the latter you are born without your own co-operation, and from it in youth you have acquired a number of ideas which will henceforth involuntarily give colour to everything.   The spiritual home, on the contrary, you have formed for yourself with full consciousness.   You therefore shape your opinions when going out from it in the full, unprejudiced light of freedom.   This formation of a spiritual home is known in the speech of occult science as "the building of the hut."

The spiritual outlook at this point extends at first to the spiritual counterparts of the physical world, so far as these lie in what we call the astral world.   In this world is found everything which in its nature is akin to human impulse, feeling, desire, or passion.   For in every sense-object that surrounds a person there are forces which are related to these human forces.   A crystal, for instance, is

formed by powers which, when seen from
the higher standpoint, are perceptible as
akin to the impulse which acts in the
human being. By similar forces the sap
is drawn through the vessels of the plant,
the blossoms unfold, the seed-cases are
made to burst. All these powers acquire
form and colour for the developed spiritual
perceptions, just as the objects of the
physical world have colour and form for
physical eyes. At the stage of development here described the student no longer
sees merely the crystal or the plant, but
likewise the spiritual forces behind them,
even as he does not now see the impulses
of animal or human being only through
their external manifestations, but also
directly as veritable objects, as in the
physical world he can see chairs and
tables. The entire world of instinct, impulse, wish or passion, whether of a person or of an animal, is there in the astral

cloud, in the aura with which the subject is enwrapt.

Besides this, the clairvoyant at this stage of his evolution perceives things that are almost or entirely withdrawn from the perceptions of sense. For example, he can observe the astral difference between a place which is for the most part filled with persons of low development and another which is inhabited by high-minded people. In a hospital it is not only the physical but also the astral atmosphere which is other than that of the ball-room. A commercial town has a different astral air from that of a university town. At first the powers of perceiving such things will be but weak in the person who has become clairvoyant. At first it will seem to be connected with the objects concerned, very much as is the dream-consciousness of the ordinary person in relation to his waking consciousness, but gradually he will completely awaken on this plane also.

The highest acquisition that comes to the clairvoyant, when he has reached this degree of sight, is that by which the astral reaction of animal or human impulses or passions is revealed to him. A loving action has quite a different astral appearance from one which proceeds out of hatred. The sensual appetite gives rise to a horrible astral image, and the feeling that is based on lofty things to one that is beautiful. These correspondences or astral pictures are only to be seen faintly during physical human life, for their strength is much lessened by existence in the physical world. A wish for any object displays itself, for instance, as a reflection of the object itself, in addition to that which the wish appears to be in the astral world. If, however, that wish is satisfied by the attainment of the

7

physical object, or if at least the possibility of such satisfaction is present, the corresponding image would only make a very faint appearance. It first comes into its full power after the death of a person, when the soul, according to its nature, continues to foster such desires, but cannot any longer satisfy them because the object and its own physical organs are both lacking. Thus the gourmet will still have the desire to tickle his palate; but the possibility of satisfaction is absent, since he no longer possesses a palate. As a result of this the desire is displayed as an exceptionally powerful image by which the soul is tormented. These experiences after death among the images of the lower soul-nature are known as the period in "Kamaloka," that is to say, in the region of desire. They only vanish away when the soul has cleansed itself from all appetites which are directed towards the physical world. Then does the soul mount up into a loftier region which is called "Devachan." Although these images are thus weak in the person who is yet alive, they still exist and follow him as his own environment in Kamaloka, just as the comet is followed by its tail, and they can be seen by the clairvoyant who has arrived at this stage of development.

Among such experiences and all that are akin to them the occult student lives in the world that has been described. He cannot as yet bring himself into touch with still loftier spiritual adventures. From this point he must climb upward still higher.

IV

THE THREE STATES OF CONSCIOUSNESS

THE life of man is passed in three states, which are as follows: waking, dreaming sleep, and dreamless deep sleep. One may comprehend how to attain to a higher knowledge of the spiritual worlds by forming an idea of the changes in the conditions that have to be undergone by the aspirant to such knowledge. Before a person has passed through the necessary training, his consciousness is continually broken by the periods of rest which accompany sleep. During these periods the soul knows nothing of the outer world

100

and nothing either of itself. Only at certain times above the wide ocean of unconsciousness there will arise dreams which are related to events in the outside world or to the conditions of the physical body. At first one recognises in dreams only a special manifestation of the sleep-existence, and commonly men speak of two states only—waking and sleeping. From the occult standpoint, however, dreams have a special significance, apart from both the other two states. It has already been shown in a previous chapter how changes occur in the dream-existence of the person who undertakes the ascent to higher knowledge. His dreams lose their meaningless, disorderly, and illogical character, and begin gradually to form a regulated, correlated world. With continued development this new world, born of one's dreams, will yield nothing to outer and phenomenal realities, not only as regards its inner truth, but also in the facts which it reveals, for these in the fullest sense of the word present a higher reality. In the phenomenal world especially there are secrets and riddles hidden everywhere. This world reveals admirably the effects of certain higher facts, but he who limits his perceptions to the senses alone cannot penetrate into causes. To the occult student such causes are partly revealed in the state already described as being evolved out of his dream-existence. To be sure, he ought not to regard these revelations as actual knowledge so long as the same things do not reveal themselves to him during ordinary waking life as well. But to that he also attains. He acquires the power to enter the state which he had first evolved from his dream-life during the hours of waking consciousness. Then the phenomenal world is enriched for him by something quite new. Just as a person who, though born blind, undergoes an operation on his sight and finds everything in his environment enriched by the new testimony of visual perception, so does the person who has become clairvoyant in the above manner, regard the entire world around him, perceiving in it new characteristics, new beings, and new things. No longer is it necessary that he should wait for a dream in order that he may live in another world, for he can transport himself into the state of higher perception at any suitable time. This condition or state has an importance for him comparable to that of perception with open eyes as opposed to a blindfold state. One can say quite literally that the occult student opens the eyes of his soul and sees things which must ever remain veiled from the bodily senses.

This state (which has previously been

described in detail) only forms the bridge
to a still higher stage of occult knowledge.
If the exercises which are assigned to him
should be continued, the student will discover at the appropriate time that the
vigorous changes hitherto mentioned affect
not only his dream-life, but that the transformation extends even to what was before
a deep and dreamless sleep. He notices
that the utter unconsciousness in which he
has always found himself during this sleep
is now broken by conscious isolated experiences. Out of the great darkness of
sleep arise perceptions of a kind which he
had never known before. Naturally it is
no easy matter to describe these perceptions, for our language is only adapted to
the phenomenal world, and in consequence
it is only possible to find approximate
words to describe what does not appertain
to that world at all. Still, one has to make
use of these words in describing the higher

worlds, and this can only be done by the free use of simile; yet, seeing that everything in the world is interrelated, such an attempt can be made. The things and beings of the higher worlds are anyway so distantly connected with those of the phenomenal world that though in good faith a portrayal of these higher worlds in the words usually descriptive of the phenomenal world may be attempted, one must always retain the idea that very much in descriptions of this kind must obviously partake of the nature of simile and imagery. Occult education itself is only partially carried on by the use of ordinary language; for the rest, the student learns in his ascent a special symbolical language, an emblematical method of expression; but nothing concerning this can at present, and for very good reasons, be openly imparted. The student must acquire it for himself in the occult school. This, however, need form no obstacle to the acquisition of some knowledge concerning the nature of the higher worlds by means of an ordinary description, such as will here be given.

If we wish to give some suggestion of the experiences mentioned above as appearing from out of the sea of unconsciousness during the period of deep sleep, we may best liken them to those of hearing. We can speak of perceptible sounds and words. If we may liken the experiences of dreaming sleep to a certain kind of seeing comparable to the perceptions of the eyes, the experiences of deep sleep allow of similar comparison with oral impressions. It may be remarked in passing that of these two faculties that of sight remains the higher even in the spiritual worlds. Colours are there still higher than sounds or words, but the student at the beginning of his development does not perceive these higher colours, but merely the inferior sounds. Only because the individual, after his general development, is already qualified for the world which reveals itself to him in dreaming sleep does he straightway perceive its colours, but he is still un-qualified for the higher world which is kindled in deep sleep, and in consequence this world reveals itself to him at first as sounds and words; later on he can mount up, here as elsewhere, to the perception of colours and forms.

If the student now realises that he passes through such experiences in deep sleep, his next task is to make them as clear and vivid as possible. In the beginning this is very difficult, for remem-brance during the waking state is at first extraordinarily scanty. You know well on waking that you have experienced some-thing; but as to its nature you remain completely in obscurity. The most important thing during the beginning of this state is that you should remain peaceful and composed, and should not allow yourself, even for a moment, to lapse into any unrest or impatience. Under all circumstances the latter condition is injurious. It can never accelerate any further development, but in every case must delay it. You must abandon yourself calmly, as it were, to what is given to you : all violence must be repressed. If at any period you cannot recall these experiences during the deep sleep, you should wait patiently until it becomes possible to do so, for such a moment will certainly some day arrive. If you have previously been patient and calm, the faculty of remembrance, when it comes, will be a securer possession ; while, should it for once appear, perhaps in answer to forcible methods, it would only mean that for a

much longer period it would afterwards
remain entirely lost.

If the power of remembrance has once
appeared and the experiences of sleep
emerge complete, vivid, and clear before
the waking consciousness, attention should
then be directed to what here follows.
Among these experiences, we can clearly
distinguish two kinds. The first kind is
totally foreign to everything that one has
ever experienced. At first one may take
pleasure in these, may let oneself be
exalted by them; but after a while they
are put aside. They are the first
harbingers of a higher spiritual world to
which one only becomes accustomed at
a later period. The other kind of experiences, however, will reveal to the
attentive observer a peculiar relationship
to the ordinary world in which he lives.
Concerning those elements of life on which
he ponders, those things in his environ-

ment which he would like to understand, but is unable to understand with the ordinary intellect, these experiences during sleep can give him information. During his daily life man reflects on that which surrounds him and he arrives at conceptions which make comprehensible to him the interrelation of things. He tries to understand in thought what he perceives with sense. It is with such ideas and conceptions that the sleep-experiences are concerned. That which was hitherto merely a dark and crepuscular conception now assumes a sonorous and vital character which can only be compared to the sounds and words of the phenomenal world. It seems to the student ever more and more that the solution of the riddle upon which he ponders is whispered in sounds and words that proceed from a finer world. Then ought he to relate what has come to him in this way with the matters of ordinary

life. What was hitherto only accessible
to his thought has now become an actual
experience for him, living and significant
as can seldom, if ever, be the case with an
experience in the world of sense. The
things and beings of the phenomenal
world are shown thereby to be more than
merely what they seem to the perceptions
of the senses. They are the expression
and the efflux of a spiritual world. This
spiritual world which lay hitherto obscure
now reveals itself to the occult student in
the whole of his environment.

It is easy to see that the possession of
this perceptive faculty can only prove
itself to be a blessing if the soul-senses of
the person in whom they have been opened
are in perfect order, just as we can only
use our ordinary senses for the accurate
observation of the world if they are in
a well-regulated condition. Now these
higher senses are formed by the individual

himself in accordance with exercises which are given to him in the course of his occult training. As much concerning these exercises as may be openly said has been already given in *The Way of Initiation.* The rest is imparted by word of mouth in the occult schools. Among these exercises we find concentration, or the directing of attention upon certain definite ideas and conceptions that are connected with the secrets of the universe; and meditation, or the living within such ideas, the complete submerging of oneself within them in the manner already explained. By concentration and meditation a person works upon his own soul and develops within it the soul-organs of perception. While he applies himself to the practice of meditation and concentration his soul evolves within his body as the embryo child grows in the body of the mother. When, during sleep, the specific experiences above described begin to occur, the moment of birth has arrived for the full-grown soul, who has thereby become literally a new being brought by the individual from seed to fruit. Instructions concerning the subject of meditation and concentration must therefore be very carefully prepared and equally carefully followed out, since they are the very laws which determine the germination and evolution of the higher soul-nature of the individual; and this must appear at its birth as a harmonious and well-formed organism. If, on the contrary, there were something lacking in these instructions, no such being would appear, but in its place one that was misborn from the standpoint of spiritual matters, and incapable of life.

That the birth of this higher soul-nature should occur during deep sleep will not seem hard of comprehension if we

8

consider that the tender organism, still unable to withstand much opposition, could hardly make itself noticed by a chance apparition among the powerful, harsh events of workaday life. Its activity cannot be observed when opposed by the activity of the body. In sleep, however, when the body is at rest, the activity of the higher soul, at first so faint and un-apparent, can come into sight in so far as it depends upon the perception of sense. A warning must here again be given that the occult student should not regard these sleep-experiences as entirely reliable sources of knowledge so long as he is not in a position to transport himself to the plane of the awakened higher soul during waking-consciousness as well. If he has acquired this power he is able to perceive the spiritual world between and within the experiences of the day, or, in other words, can comprehend as sounds and words the hidden secrets of his surroundings.

At this period of development we must clearly understand that we are dealing, at first, with separate, more or less unconnected, spiritual experiences. We must be on our guard against the erection of any system of knowledge, whether complete or only interdependent. By so doing we should merely confuse the soul-world with all manner of fantastical ideas and conceptions; and thus we could very easily weave a world which has really no connection whatever with the true spiritual world. The occult student must practise continually the strictest self-control. The right method is to grow clearer and clearer in one's realisation of the separate and veritable experiences which occur, and then to wait for the arrival of new experiences, full and unforced in their nature, which will connect themselves, as if on their own account, with those that have already occurred. By virtue of the power of the spiritual world in which he has now once found his way, and by virtue, also, of practising the prescribed exercises, the student now experiences an ever-enlarging, ever more comprehensive, outspreading of consciousness in deep sleep. Out of what was erstwhile mere unconsciousness, more and more experiences emerge, and ever fewer and fewer become those periods in the sleep-existence that remain unconscious. Thus, then, do the separate experiences of sleep continually close in upon each other without this actual interlocking being disturbed by a multitude of combinations and inferences which would still arise from the meddling of the intellect accustomed to the phenomenal world. The less one's ordinary habits of thought are mixed up in some unauthorised manner with these higher experiences, the better it is.

If you conduct yourself rightly, you now approach nearer and nearer to that stage of the way at which the entire sleep-life is passed in complete consciousness. Then you exist, when the body is at rest, in a reality as actual as is the case while you are awake. It is superfluous to remark that during sleep we are dealing, at first, with a reality entirely different from the phenomenal environment in which the body finds itself. Indeed we learn — nay, must learn if we are to keep our footing on firm ground and avoid becoming a fantastic—to relate the higher experiences of sleep to the phenomenal environment. At first, however, the world which is entered in sleep is a completely new revelation. In occult science the important stage at which consciousness is retained interiorly through the entire sleep-life is known as the "continuity of consciousness." [1]

In the case of a person who has arrived at this point, experiences and events do not cease during the intervals when the physical body rests, and no impressions are conveyed to the soul through the medium of the senses.

[1] That which is here referred to is, at a certain stage of development, a kind of "ideal," the goal which lies at the end of a long road. The next things that the student learns are two extensions of consciousness—first, into a soul-state wherein hitherto nothing but unregulated dreams were possible, and, secondly, into another state wherein hitherto nothing was possible except unconscious and dreamless sleep. He then knows the three states, even if it remains impossible for him to refuse entirely all tribute to the ordinary state of sleep.

V

THE DISSOCIATION
OF HUMAN PERSONALITY
DURING INITIATION.

DURING deep sleep the human soul does
not register impressions through the
medium of the physical senses. In that
state the perceptions of the external world
do not touch it. It is, in truth, outside
the coarser part of human nature, the
physical body, and is only connected with
the finer bodies—known as the astral and
etheric—which escape the observation of
the physical senses. The activity of these
finer bodies does not cease in sleep. Even
as the physical body stands in a certain

119

relation to the things and beings of its own world, even as it is affected by these and affects them, so is it also with the soul in a higher world, but in this latter case, experience continues during sleep. The soul is then veritably in full activity, but we cannot know of these personal activities as long as we have no higher senses, by means of which we may observe, during sleep, what happens around us and what we do ourselves, just as well as we can use our ordinary senses in daily life for the observation of our physical environment. Occult training consists (as has been shown in the foregoing chapters) in the upbuilding of just such higher senses.

By means of examples like that which follows one can readily conceive how the soul with its finer vehicles may continue its activity during the intervals when the physical body is at rest. It is no mere nursery tale which will here be told, but

a real case from life, which was observed
with all the means possessed by the
clairvoyant investigator and with all the
care which it is incumbent upon him to
exercise; nor is it related as a " proof,"
but merely as an illustration.[1]

A young man stood confronted by an
examination which would probably decide
his entire future life. For a long time
previously, he had worked for it assidu-
ously, and consequently, on the evening

[1] It has been necessary to make this preamble, since
the superstitious followers of materialism, as soon as
they hear of any such story, immediately respond by
declaring that these cases prove nothing. They whittle
away everything of the kind as the result of delusion
and inaccurate observation. To them it should be
remarked, by way of reply, that the clairvoyant
investigator does not require such indirect proofs; he
attains to a direct knowledge by means of the higher
sight. Nevertheless, facts of the kind related above
serve to illustrate what is meant. To establish their
truth other means exist than those which materialistic
learning will use in the unimpeachable exposition of a
matter of ordinary fact.

before the examination, was exceedingly tired. He was to appear before the examiners punctually at eight in the morning of the following day. He wanted to have a night's restful sleep before the trial, but he feared lest, on account of his exhaustion, he might not be able to wake himself at the right hour. He therefore took the precaution to arrange that a person living in the next room should wake him at six o'clock by knocking at his door. Thus he was able to abandon himself to sleep with an easy mind. On the following day he awoke, not at the call of his neighbour, but out of a dream. He heard six sharp rifle-reports, and with the sixth he was awake. His watch— equipped with no alarum—stood at six o'clock. He dressed himself, and after half an hour his neighbour knocked him up. In reality, it was only just then six o'clock, for his watch, by some accident, had gained half an hour in the night. The dream which awakened him had timed itself to the erroneous watch. What was it, then, which happened here? The soul of the young man had remained active even during his sleep. Because he had previously formed a connection between this activity of soul and the watch at his side, there had remained a connection between the two for the whole of the night, so that on the next day the soul came, as it were, to the hour of six simultaneously with the watch. This activity had impressed itself on the young man's consciousness through the pictorial dream already described, which had awakened him. One cannot explain it away by reference to the increasing light of day or anything similar, for the soul acted not in accordance with the real time of day, but with the erroneous watch. The soul was active like a veritable watchman while the physical person slept. It is not the activity of the soul which is lacking in sleep, but rather a consciousness of that activity.

If, by occult training, the sleep-life of a person is cultivated, in the way already set forth in the previous chapter, he can then follow consciously everything which passes before him while in this particular state; he can voluntarily put himself *en rapport* with his environment, just as with his experiences, known through the physical senses, during the continuance of the waking consciousness. Had the young man in the above example been a clairvoyant, he would have been able to watch the time for himself during sleep, and in consequence to have awakened himself. It is necessary to state here that the perception of the ordinary phenomenal environment presupposes one of the higher stages of clairvoyance. At the beginning of his development at this stage, the student only perceives things which pertain to another world, without being able to discern their relation to the objects of his workaday surroundings.

That which is illustrated in such typical examples of dream—or sleep—life is repeatedly experienced by people. The soul lives on unintermittently in the higher worlds and is active within them. Out of those higher worlds it continually draws the suggestions upon which it works when again in the physical body, while the ordinary man remains unconscious of this higher life. It is the work of the occult student to make it conscious, and by so doing his life becomes transformed. So long as the soul has not the higher sight, it is guided by foreign agencies, and just as the life of a blind man to whom sight is given by an operation becomes quite different from what it was before, so that he can henceforth dispense with a guide, thus also does the life of a person change under the influence of occult training. He, too, is now abandoned by his guide and must henceforward guide himself. As soon as this occurs he is, of course, liable to errors of which his waking consciousness had no conception. He now deals with a world in which, hitherto and unknown to himself, he had been influenced by higher powers. These higher powers are regulated by the great universal harmony. It is from this harmony that the student emerges. He has now to accomplish for himself things which were hitherto done for him without his co-operation.

Because this is the case there will be much said in the treatises which deal with such things concerning the dangers which are connected with an ascent into the higher worlds. The descriptions of these dangers which have sometimes been given are very apt to make timid souls regard this higher life only with horror. It should here be said that these experiences only occur if the necessary rules of prudence are neglected. On the other hand, if everything which a genuine occult education imparts as counsel were here given as a warning, it would be manifest that the ascent is through experiences which in magnitude, as in form, surpass everything that has been painted by the boldest fancy of an ordinary person; yet it is not reasonable to talk of possible injury to health or life. The student learns to recognise horrible threatening forms that haunt every corner and cranny of life. It is even possible for him to make use of such powers and beings who are withdrawn from the perceptions of sense, and the temptation to use these powers in the service of some forbidden interest of his own is very great.   There is also the possibility of employing these forces in erroneous ways, owing to an inadequate knowledge concerning the higher worlds. Some of these especially important events (as, for example, the meeting with " the Guardian of the Threshold ") will be described further on in this treatise.   Yet one must realise that these hostile powers are around us even when we do not know anything about them.   It is true that in this case their relation to man is determined by higher powers, and that this relationship only changes when he consciously enters the world which was hitherto unknown to him.   At the same time, this will enhance his existence and enlarge the circle of his life to an enormous extent.   There is danger only if the student, whether from impatience or arrogance, assumes too early an independence in his attitude toward the experiences of the higher world—if he cannot wait until he acquires a really mature insight into superphysical laws.   In this sphere the words "humility" and "modesty" are still less empty than in ordinary life.   If these, in the very best sense, are the attributes of the student, he may be sure that his ascent into the higher life may be achieved without any danger to what one usually means by health and life.   Above all things it is needful that there should be no disharmony between these higher experiences and the events and demands of every-day life.   The student's task throughout is to search on earth, and he who tries to withdraw from the sacred tasks of this earth and to escape into another world may be sure that he never reaches his goal. Yet what the senses behold is only a part of the world, and in spiritual regions lie the causes of what are facts in the

9

phenomenal world. One should partici-
pate in the things of the spirit in order to
carry one's revelations into the world of
the senses. Man transforms the earth,
by implanting in it that which he has
discovered in the spiritual world, and that
is his task. Yet, because the earth is
dependent upon the spiritual world—
because we can only be truly effective on
earth if we have part in those worlds
wherein lie concealed the creative forces—
we ought to be willing to ascend into those
regions. If a person enters on a course
of occult training with this sentiment, and
if he never deviates for a moment from
the directions already given, he has not
even the most insignificant of dangers to
fear. No one ought to hold back from
occult education on account of the dangers
that confront him ; rather should the very
prospect form a powerful inducement
toward the acquisition of those qualities

which must be possessed by the genuine occult student.

After these preliminaries, which ought certainly to dispel all forebodings, let us now describe one of these "dangers." It is true that very considerable changes are undergone by the finer bodies of the occult student. These changes are connected with certain evolutionary events which happen within the three fundamental forces of the soul—the will, the feelings, and the thoughts. As regards the occult training of a person these three forces stand in a definite relation, regulated by the laws of the higher world. He does not will, nor think, nor feel, in an arbitrary manner. If, for example, a particular idea arises in his mind, then, in accordance with natural laws, a certain feeling is attached to it, or else it is followed by a resolution of the will that is likewise connected with it according to law. You enter a room, find it to be stuffy, and open the window. You hear your name called, and follow the call. You are questioned and you answer. You perceive an ill-smelling object and you experience a feeling of disgust. These are simple connections between thought, feeling, and will. If, however, the student surveys human life, he will observe that everything in it is built up on such connections. Indeed, we only call the life of a person "normal" if we detect in it just that interrelation of thought, feeling, and will which is founded on the laws of human nature. We deem it contrary to these laws if a person, for instance, takes pleasure in an ill-smelling object, or if, on being questioned, he does not answer. The success which we expect from a right education or a fitting instruction consists in our presupposition that we can thereby impart to our pupil an interrelation of

thought, feeling, and will that corresponds
to human nature. When we present to
a pupil any particular ideas, we do so on
the supposition that they will assimilate,
in an orderly association, with his feelings
and volitions. All this arises from the
fact that in the finer soul-vehicles of man
the central points of the three powers,
feeling, thinking, and willing, are connected with each other in a definite way.
This connection in the finer soul-vehicles
has also its analogy in the coarse physical
body. There, too, the organs of volition
stand in a certain orderly relation to those
of thinking and feeling. A definite
thought regularly evokes a feeling or a
volition. In the course of a person's higher
development the threads which connect
these three principles with each other are
severed. At first this rupture occurs only
in regard to the finer organism of the soul;
but at a still higher stage the separation

extends also to the physical body.   In
the higher spiritual evolution of a person
his brain actually divides into three
separated parts.   The separation, indeed,
is of such a nature that it is not perceptible to ordinary sense-observation,
nor could it be detected by the keenest
physical instruments.   Yet it occurs, and
the clairvoyant has means of observing
it.   The brain of the higher clairvoyant
divides into three independent active
entities : the thought-brain, the feeling-
brain, and the willing-brain.

The organs of thinking, feeling, and
willing remain, then, quite free in themselves, and their connection is no longer
maintained by a law innate in them, but
must now be tended by the growing higher
consciousness of the individual.   This,
then, is the change which the occult
student observes coming over himself—
that there is no longer a connection

between a thought and a feeling, or a feeling and a volition, except when he creates the connection himself. No impulse drives him from thought to action if he does not voluntarily harbour it. He can now stand completely without feeling before an object which, before his training, would have filled him with glowing love or violent hatred; he can likewise remain actionless before a thought which heretofore would have spurred him on to action as if by itself. He can execute deeds by an effort of will where not the remotest cause would be visible to a person who had not been through the occult school. The greatest acquisition which the occult student inherits is the attainment of complete lordship over the connecting threads of the three powers of the soul; yet simultaneously these connections are placed entirely at his own responsibility.

Only through such alterations in his

nature can a person come into conscious touch with certain superphysical powers and entities. For between his own soul and certain fundamental forces of the world there are correspondences or links. The power, for instance, which lies in the will can act upon, and perceive, particular things and entities of the higher world, but it can only do so when dissociated from the threads that link it with the feelings and thoughts of the soul. As soon as this separation is effected the activities of the will can be manifested, and so is it likewise with the forces of thought and feeling. If a person sends out a feeling of hatred, it is visible to the clairvoyant as a thin cloud of light of a special hue, and the clairvoyant can ward off such a feeling, just as an ordinary person wards off a physical blow that is aimed at him. Hate is a perceptible phenomenon in the superphysical world, but the clairvoyant is only able to perceive it in so far as he can send out the force which resides in his feelings, just as an ordinary person can direct outwards the receptive faculty of his eyes. What is here applied to hatred applies also to far more important facts in the phenomenal world. The individual can come into conscious communion with them by this very liberation of the elemental forces in the soul.

On account of this division of the thinking, feeling, and willing forces it is now possible that a threefold error may overtake the development of a person who has been disregardful of his occult instructions. Such an error might occur if the connecting threads were severed before the student had acquired so much knowledge of the higher consciousness as would enable him to hold the reins by which to guide well, such as a free, harmonious

co-operation of the separate forces would
supply. For, as a rule, the three human
principles at any given period of life are
not symmetrically developed. In one the
power of thought is advanced beyond
those of feeling and will; in a second,
another power has the upper hand over
its companions. So long as the connection between these forces—a connection
produced by the laws of the higher world
—remains intact, no injurious irregularity,
in the higher sense, can result from the
predominance of one force or another.
In a person of will-power, for instance,
thought and feeling work by those laws
to equalise all and to prevent the over-
weighty will from falling into a kind of
degeneration. If such a person, however,
should take up an occult training, the law-
given influence of thought and feeling
upon the monstrous, unchecked, oppressive
will would entirely cease. If, then, the

individual has not carried his control of the higher consciousness so far that he can call up the desirable harmony for himself, the will continues on its own unbridled way and repeatedly overpowers its possessor. Thought and feeling lapse into complete debility; and the individual is whipped like a slave by his own over-mastering will. A violent nature which rushes from one uncurbed action to another is the result.

A second deviation ensues if feeling shakes off its appropriate bridle in the same extreme manner. A person who bows in adoration before another may easily give himself over to an unlimited dependence, until his own thought and will are ruined. In place of the higher knowledge a pitiful vacuity and feebleness would become the lot of such a person. Again, in a case where feeling largely preponderates, a nature too much given over to piety and religious aspiration may lapse into religious extravagance that carries him away.

The third evil is found where thought is too prominent, for then there may result a contemplative nature inimical to life and shut within itself. To such persons the world only appears to have any significance so far as it offers them objects for the satisfaction of their limitless thirst for wisdom. They are never impelled by a thought either to a feeling or to a deed. They are seen at once to be cold, unfeeling folk. They fly away from every contact with the things of ordinary life as from something that stings them to aversion, or that at least has lost all meaning for them.

These are the three ways of error against which the occult student should be counselled : over-action, excess of feeling, and a cold, unloving struggle after wisdom. Viewed from without—as also from the materialistic medical standpoint —the picture of an occult student upon one of these byways does not greatly differ (especially in degree) from that of a madman, or at least of a person suffering from severe nervous illness.   From all this it will be clear how important it is to occult education that the three principles of the soul should throughout be symmetrically developed, before their innate connection is severed and the awakened higher consciousness enthroned in its place; for if a mistake once occurs, if one of these principles falls into lawlessness, the higher soul appears as a thing misborn.   The unbridled force then pervades the individual's entire personality; and one cannot expect the balance to be restored for a long time.   That which seems but a harmless characteristic so long as its possessor is without occult training,—especially if he belongs to the willing, thinking, or feeling type,—is so increased in the occult student that the more homely virtues, so necessary for everyday life, are apt to be obscured.

A really serious danger is at hand when the student has acquired the faculty of calling up before him in waking consciousness those things that he can experience in the state of sleep. As long as it is only a matter of illuminating the intervals of sleep, the sense-life, regulated according to common universal laws, always works during the waking hours towards restoring the disturbed equilibrium of the soul. That is why it is so essential that the waking life of an occult student should in every respect be healthy and systematic. The more he fulfils the demand which is made by the external world upon a sound and powerful type of body, soul, and spirit, the better it is for him. On the other hand, it may be very

bad for him if his ordinary waking life
acts so as to excite or irritate him; if any
disturbing or hindering influence from
the external life occurs during the great
changes that are undergone by his inner
nature. He should seek for everything
which corresponds to his powers and
faculties, everything that puts him in an
undisturbed harmonious connection with
his environment. He should avoid everything which upsets this harmony, everything that brings unrest and fever into his
life. Regarding this, it is not so much a
matter of removing this unrest or fever in
an external sense, as of taking care that
the moods, purposes, thoughts, and bodily
health do not thereby undergo a continual
fluctuation. During his occult training
all this is not so easy for a person to
accomplish as it was before, since the
higher experiences, which are now interwoven with his life, react uninterruptedly

upon his entire existence. If something in these higher experiences is not in its place, the irregularity lurks perpetually and is liable to throw him off the right path at every turn. For this reason the student should omit nothing which will secure for him a lasting control over his entire nature, nor should presence of mind, and a peaceful survey of all possible situations in life ever be allowed to desert him. A genuine occult training, indeed, itself engenders all these attributes, and in the course of such training one only learns to know these dangers at the precise moment when one acquires the full power to rout them from the field.

VI

THE FIRST GUARDIAN OF THE THRESHOLD

AMONG the important experiences that accompany an ascent into the higher worlds is that of "Meeting with the Guardian of the Threshold." In reality there is not only one such Guardian, but two; one known as "the Lesser," the other as "the Greater." The student meets with the former when, in the manner described in the last chapter, he begins to loosen the connection between the volitions, the thoughts, and the feelings so far as they concern the etheric and astral bodies. The meeting with the Greater

Guardian occurs when this loosening of the links further extends to the physical body (that is to say, the brain).

The Lesser Guardian of the Threshold is an independent being. It did not exist before the individual had arrived at this particular point in his evolution. It is the individual's creation. Only one of its essential functions can be here described,—indeed it were no easy matter to furnish a complete description.

First of all, let us present in narrative form the meeting of the occult student with the Guardian of the Threshold. Only by means of this meeting does the former become aware of the separation of the threads that connected his thoughts, his volitions, and his feelings.

A terrible spectral creature, in truth, is this that confronts the student. The latter needs all the presence of mind and all the faith in the security of his way to wisdom which he could acquire during his previous training.

The Guardian proclaims his significance in something like these words:—"Hitherto, powers which were invisible to you have watched over you. They worked so that in the course of your life your good deeds brought their reward, your evil actions their disastrous results. Through their influence your character formed itself out of your experiences and your thoughts. They were the instruments of your fate. It was they that ordered the measure of joy and pain which was meted out to you in any one of your incarnations, according to your conduct in earlier lives. They ruled you by the all-binding law of Karma. Now they shall free you from a part of their constraint, and a portion of that which they have accomplished for you must you now accomplish for yourself. In the past you have borne many hard blows from Fate. Did you not know wherefore? Each was the effect of a pernicious deed in a life gone by. You found joy and gladness, and you partook of them. They, too, were the fruits of earlier deeds. In your character you have many beautiful qualities, many ugly flaws; and both of these you have woven for yourself out of your bygone experiences and thoughts. Till now you did not know of this; only the effects were revealed to you. But they, the Karmic Powers, beheld all the deeds of your former lives, all your obscure thoughts and feelings; and thus have they determined what you now are and the manner in which you now live.

"But the hour has come when all the good and the evil aspects of your bygone lives shall be laid open before you. Till now they were interwoven with your whole being; they were in you, and you

could not see them, even as with physical
eyes you cannot see your own physical
brain.   Now, however, they detach themselves from you ; they emerge from your
personality.   They assume an independent form which you can observe, even
as you observe the stones and flowers of
the external world.   And I—I am that
very being which has found for itself a
body wrought of your noble and your
ignoble deeds.   My spectral robe is woven
according to the entries in your life's
ledger.   Hitherto you have borne me
invisibly within yourself, yet it was well
for you that this should be, for the wisdom
of the destiny which was hidden even
from yourself has therefore worked
hitherto toward the extinguishing of the
hideous stains that were upon my form.
Now that I have emerged, that hidden
wisdom also departs from you.   It will
henceforth trouble itself no more concern-

ing you. It will now leave the work in
your hands alone. It is for me to become
a complete and splendid being, if I am
not, indeed, to fall into decay. If this,
the latter, should occur, then should I
drag you also down into a dark and ruined
world. If you would avoid this, then let
your own wisdom become so great that it
can take over to itself the task of that
other wisdom which was hidden from you,
and is now departed. When you have
passed my threshold I shall never leave
your side for a single moment. From
henceforth, when you do or think anything
that is evil, you will straightway discern
your guilt as a hideous, demoniacal distor-
tion of this that is my form. Only when
you have made good all your bygone evil
deeds and have so elevated yourself that
further evil becomes a thing impossible to
you,—only then will my being be transformed into glorious beauty. Then, too,

shall I again unite myself with you in one being for the helping of your further activity.

"My threshold is constructed out of every feeling of fear to which you are still accessible, out of every shrinking from the power which will take over to itself the complete responsibility for all your deeds and thoughts. So long as you have still any fear of that self-government of your fate, all that belongs to this threshold has not yet been built into it; and so long as a single stone is there found missing, you must remain standing as one forbidden entrance, or else must you stumble. Seek not, then, to pass my threshold until you feel yourself liberated from all fear, ready for the highest responsibility.

"Hitherto I have only emerged from your personality when Death recalled you from an earthly life, but even then my form was veiled from you. Only the

powers of destiny who watched over you
could behold me, and they were able, in
accordance with my appearance, to build
in you, during the interval between death
and a new birth, all that power and that
capacity wherewith in a new terrestrial
existence you could labour at the glorifying of my form for the assurance of your
progress. It was on account of my imperfection, indeed, that the powers of
destiny were driven again and again to
lead you back into a new incarnation upon
earth. If you died, I was yet there; and
according to me did the Lords of Karma
fashion the manner of your re-birth.

"Only when through an endless proces-
sion of lives you have brought me to perfection shall you no longer descend among
the powers of death, but, having united
yourself absolutely with me, you shall pass
over with me into immortality.

"Thus do I stand before you here to-day

visible, as I have always stood invisible beside you in the hour of death. When you shall have passed my threshold you will enter those kingdoms which else would have opened to you only at physical death. You will enter them with full knowledge, and henceforth, when you wander outwardly visible upon the earth, you will also move through the kingdom of death, which is the kingdom of eternal life. I am indeed the angel of Death; yet at the same time I am the bringer of an imperishable higher life. Through me you will die while still living in your body, to be reborn into an immortal existence.

"The kingdom that you now enter will introduce you to beings of a superhuman kind, and in that kingdom happiness will be your lot. But the first acquaintance to be made in that world must be myself, I that am your own creation. Erstwhile I lived upon your life, but now through you I have grown to a separate existence and here stand before you as the visible gauge of your future deeds, perhaps, too, as your constant reproach. You were able to form me, but in so doing you have taken up the duty of transforming me."

What has been here presented in a narrative form one must not imagine to be merely something allegorical, but realise that it is an experience of the student which is in the highest degree actual.[1] The Guardian will warn him not to go

---

[1] It will be divined from the above that the Guardian of the Threshold there described is an (astral) form, such as is revealed to the awakened higher sight of the occult student, and it is to this superphysical "meeting" that occult science conducts. It is one of the lesser magical performances to make the Guardian of the Threshold visible on the physical plane also. To make this possible it is necessary to produce a cloud of smoke, consisting of fine substances, by means of some frankincense which is composed of a number of ingredients in a particular

further if he does not feel in himself the power necessary for the fulfilment of those demands which have been set forth in the preceding speech. ⸗ Although the form of the Guardian is so frightful, it is yet nothing but the effect of the student's own past lives, his own character, risen out of him into an independent life.   This awakening is brought about by the mutual separation of the volitions, the thoughts, and the feelings.   It is an experience of the deepest significance when one feels for the first time that one has produced a

commixture. The developed power of the magician is then able to mould the smoke into shape and to animate its substance with the still unbalanced Karma of the individual. He who is sufficiently prepared for the higher vision no longer requires this pheno- menal sight, while he who sees his still unbalanced Karma, without adequate preparation, as a visible living creature before his eyes, exposes himself to the greatest danger of falling into evil byways. The Guardian of the Threshold has been romantically depicted by Bulwer Lytton in *Zanoni*.

spiritual being. The next thing to be aimed at is the preparation of the occult student so that he can endure the terrible sight without a vestige of timidity, and at the moment of the meeting really feel his power to be so increased that he can take it upon himself to effect with full realisation the glorifying of the Guardian.

A result of this meeting with the Guardian of the Threshold, if successful, is that the next physical death of the student is an event entirely different from what death was before. He consciously goes through the death whereby he lays aside the physical body, as he lays aside an outworn garment or one that is grown useless on account of a sudden rent. This —his physical death—is now only an important fact, as it were, to those who have lived with him, whose preceptions are still restricted to the world of the senses. For them the occult student " dies," but for himself nothing of importance in his whole environment is changed. The entire superphysical world into which he steps already stood open to him before death, and it is the same world that after death confronts him.

Now, the Guardian of the Threshold is also connected with other matters. The individual belongs to a family, a nation, a race. His deeds in this world depend upon his relationship to this greater unit. His individual character is likewise connected with it. The conscious deeds of a single person are by no means the sum of all he must reckon with in respect of his family, stock, nation, and race. There is a destiny, as there is a character, pertaining to the family or the race or the nation. For the person who is restricted to his senses these things remain as general ideas, and the materialistic thinker will regard the occult scientist contemptuously when he hears that for the latter the family or national character, the lineal or racial destiny, becomes just as real a being as the personality which is produced by the character and destiny of the individual. The occultist comes to know of higher worlds in which the separated personalities are discerned as members, like the arms, legs, and head of an individual; and in the life of a family, of a nation, or a race, he sees at work not only the separate individuals, but also the very real souls of the family, nation, or race. Indeed, in a certain sense, the separate individuals are only the executive organs of this family or racial spirit. In truth, one can say that the soul of a nation, for example, makes use of an individual belonging to that nation, for the execution of certain deeds. The national soul does not descend to sensible reality. It dwells in higher worlds, and in order to work in the physical world makes use of the physical organs of a particular person. In a higher sense it is as when an architect makes use of a workman for executing the details of a building. Every person gets his work assigned him, in the truest sense of the words, by the soul of the family, the nation, or the race. Now the ordinary person is by no means initiated into the higher scheme of his work. He works unconsciously toward the goal of the nation or race. From the moment when the occult student meets the Guardian of the Threshold, he has not merely to discern his own tasks as a personality, but must also work consciously at those of his nation or his race. Every extension of his horizon implies an extension of his duties. As a matter of fact, the occult student joins a new body to those finer vehicles of his soul. He puts on another garment. Hitherto he went through the world with those coverings which clothed his personality. That which he must accomplish for his community, his nation, or his race, is managed by the higher spirits which utilise his personality. A further revelation which is now made to him by the Guardian is that henceforth these spirits will withdraw their hands from him. He must get quite clear of that union. Now, if he did not develop in himself those powers which pertain to the national or racial spirits, he would completely harden himself as a separate creature and would rush upon his own destruction. Doubtless there are many people who would say, " Oh ! I have entirely freed myself from all lineal or racial connections ; I only want to be man and nothing but man." To these one must reply, " Who, then, brought you to this freedom ? Was it not your family who gave you that position in the world where you now stand? Was it not your ancestry, your nation, your race, that have made you what you are? They have brought you up; and if you are now exalted above all prejudices, if you are one of the light-bringers and benefactors of your clan, or even of your race, you owe that to their education. Indeed, when you say of yourself that you are 'nothing as a person,' you owe the very fact that you have so become to the spirit of your community." Only the occult student learns what it means to be cut off entirely from the family, the clan, or the racial spirit. He alone realises the insignificance of all such education in respect of the life which now confronts him, for everything that has gathered around him falls utterly away when the threads that bind the will, the thoughts, and the feelings are sundered. He looks back on

11

all the events of his previous education as one must regard a house of which the stones have fallen apart in pieces and which one must therefore build up again in a new form.

It is more than merely a figure of speech to say that after the Guardian of the Threshold has uttered his first communications, there rises up from the place where he stands a great whirlwind, which extinguishes all those lights of the spirit which had hitherto illumined the pathway of life. At the same time an utter blackness engulfs the student. It is only broken a little by the rays that stream forth from the Guardian of the Threshold, and out of that darkness resound his last admonitions :—"Step not across my threshold before you are assured that you can illuminate the blackness by yourself : take not a single step forward unless you are certain that you have a sufficiency of oil in your lamp. The lamps of the guides which hitherto you have followed will now, in the future, be absent." After these words the student has to turn round and direct his gaze backward. The Guardian of the Threshold now draws away a veil that before had hidden deep secrets. The lineal, the national, the racial spirits are revealed in their complete reality, and the student now sees clearly how he had been guided so far, but it also dawns upon him that henceforth he will have no such guidance. This is a second warning received at the threshold from its guardian.

No one can attain to this vision unprepared; but the higher training, which generally makes it possible for a person to press on to the threshold, puts him simultaneously in a position to find at the right moment the necessary power. Indeed, this training is of so harmonious a kind, that the entrance into the new life can be made to lose its exciting and tumultuous character. The experience at the threshold is, for the occult student, attended by a foreshadowing of that bliss which is to form the keynote of his newly awakened life. The sensation of a new freedom will outweigh all other feelings ; and together with this sensation the new duties and the new responsibilities will seem as something which must needs be undertaken by a person at a particular stage in his life.

VII

THE SECOND GUARDIAN OF
THE THRESHOLD

LIFE AND DEATH

IT has already been shown how important for the individual is the meeting
with the so-called Lesser Guardian of
the Threshold, because he then becomes
aware of a superphysical being which he
has himself created. The body of this
being is constructed out of the results—
hitherto imperceptible to him—of his
actions, feelings, and thoughts. It is
these invisible forces that have become
the cause of his destiny and his character.
It is then clear to the individual that in

the past he himself laid the ground-plans for the present. His nature now stands revealed, to a certain extent, before him. For instance, it comprises particular inclinations and habits. He can now understand why he has them. He has met with certain blows of fate; he now knows whence they came. He perceives why he loves one and hates another; why he is made happy by this and unhappy by that. By means of the invisible causes the visible life is made comprehensible. The essential facts of life, too, such as illness and health, death and birth, unveil themselves before his gaze. He observes how he had woven before his birth the causes which necessitated his return to life. From thenceforth he knows that being within himself which is constructed in the visible world after an imperfect manner, and which can only be brought to perfection in the same visible world;

for in no other world is there the opportunity of working at the upbuilding of that being. Further than this, he sees how death cannot sever him lastingly from this world. For he should say to himself: "Once I came for the first time to this world because I was a being that needed the life here lived in order to evolve those attributes which could not be developed in any other world. Here must I remain until I have evolved in myself whatever can here be attained. I shall only become, at some far-off time, a fit worker in another world if I have developed in the phenomenal world all the qualities which pertain to it."

Among the most important experiences of the Initiate is that which occurs when he first learns to know and to cherish the visible world at its true value; and this knowledge comes to him by his very insight into the superphysical world. He who cannot see there and who consequently imagines that the superphysical worlds are infinitely the more valuable, is likely to under-estimate the worth of the phenomenal world. He, however, who has had that insight into the superphysical worlds well knows that without his experiences in the visible he would be totally powerless in the invisible. If he would really live in the latter he must possess the faculties and instruments for that life, and these he can only acquire in the visible world. He must attain spiritual vision if the invisible world is to become perceptible to him; but this power of vision in a "higher" world is gradually developed through the experiences of the "lower." One can no more be born into a spiritual world with spiritual eyes, if one has not prepared them in the world of sense, than a child could be born with physical eyes if they had not already been formed in the mother's womb.

From this standpoint it will also be obvious why the " threshold " to the super-physical world is watched by a "Guardian." In no case may a true vision of that sphere be granted to a person who has not yet acquired the necessary faculties.   For this reason, at each death a veil is drawn over the realities of the other world when a person enters it while still incapable of working within it.   He should only behold them when he is ripe for it.

When the occult student enters the superphysical world, life assumes quite a new meaning to him, for in the world of sense he discerns the seed-ground of a higher world ; so that in a certain sense this " higher " will seem very defective without the " lower." Two outlooks are opened before him : the first into the Past ; the second into the Future.

He looks into a past when this visible world was not. Long ago had he outgrown the fancy that the superphysical world had developed itself out of the sense-world. He well knows that the superphysical was the first, and that out of it everything phenomenal has been evolved. He sees how he himself, before he came for the first time to this phenomenal world, belonged to a world superior to the senses. Yet this, the pristine superphysical world, needed to pass through the physical. Without such a passage its further evolution would not have been possible. Only when the beings of the phenomenal world have developed within themselves the faculties that correspond to that world can the supersensual beings again move onward. These beings are no other than men and women. They have arisen, as they now live, from an imperfect stage of spiritual existence, and must in their own inner nature bring about its completion, whereby they will then be fit for further work in the higher world. Thus begins the outlook into the future. It points to a higher stage in the supersensual world. In this will appear the fruits which have been matured in the world of sense. The latter, as such, will be superseded, but its experiences will be incorporated into a higher sphere.

Thus is revealed the *raison d'être* of illness and death in the world of sense. Death is nothing else than a sign that the former superphysical world had arrived at a point from which it could not make any further progress by itself. It would necessarily have had to undergo a universal death if it had not received a new life-impulse, and the new life has thus come down to battle with universal death. Out of the remnants of a world decaying and chilly, blossoms the seed of a new world. That is why we have death and life in the world. Slowly things pass over into each other. The decaying portion of the old world still adheres to the seeds of the new life, which indeed arose out of it. The fullest expression of this may be found among human beings. Man bears as a covering that which he has gathered about him in the old world, and within this covering is formed the germ of that being which in the future will have life. He is therefore of a double nature, mortal and immortal. In his ending state he is mortal; in his beginning state immortal; but it is only within this twofold world, which finds its expression in the physical, that he can acquire those faculties which will conduct him to the undying world. Indeed, his task is precisely to draw out of the mortal the fruits of the immortal. If he glances at his own nature, which he himself has formed in the past, he cannot but say : "I have in me the elements of a decaying world. They are at work in me, and only little by little can I break their power by means of the newly created immortal elements." Thus man goes on his way from death to life. He applies to life what he learns through death. If in full consciousness he could speak to himself in his death-hour, he might say : "Death is my teacher. The fact that I am dying is a result of the entire past wherein I am enmeshed. Yet the soil of death has matured in me the seed of what is deathless. This it is that I take with me into another world. If it had been a matter merely of the past, I should not then have been born. At birth the life of the past is closed. Life in the sense-world is rescued from an all-consuming death by the new life-germ within. The time between birth and death is only an expression for as much as the new life was able to rescue from the decaying past ; and illness is nothing else than the effect of that portion of the past which is declining."

In all that has here been said we find an answer to the question, "Why is it that only little by little and through error and imperfection may man work his way up to the good and true?" At first his actions, feelings, and thoughts are under the dominion of the fading and the mortal. From this are shaped his physical organs, and therefore these organs, and the forces which act on them, are consecrated to the perishable. The instincts, impulses, and passions, or the organs which belong to them, do not themselves manifest the imperishable, but rather will that which emerges from the work of these organs become imperishable. Only when man has worked out of the perishable everything that is to be worked out, will he rid himself of these principles from which he has grown and which find their expression in the physically perceptible world.

Thus, then, the first Guardian of the Threshold stands as the replica of the individual in his double nature, wherein are mingled the perishable and the imperishable ; and it is then made clear to him how much he lacks before he can attain the sublime form of light which may once more inhabit the pure spiritual world.

The degree in which he is enmeshed in the physical sense-nature will be shown to the student by the Guardian of the Threshold. This entanglement is expressed by the existence of instincts, impulses, appetites, egotistical desires, all forms of selfishness, and so forth. It is also expressed in the connection with a race, a nation, and so on; for nations and races are only so many different evolutionary stages up to the pure humanity.

A race or a nation stands so much the higher, the more completely it gives expression to its kinship with the type of pure and ideal humanity, the more it has worked through the physical and perishable to the superphysical and imperishable. The evolution of the individual by means of reincarnation in ever higher national and racial forms is therefore a process of liberation. Ultimately the individual will appear in his harmonious perfection. In a similar way the pilgrimage through ever purer moral and religious conceptions is a perfecting process. Every moral stage, for instance, still retains, beside the idealistic germ of the future, a passion for the perishable.

Now in the Guardian of the Threshold, above described, only the result of time that has passed away is manifested, and in the germ of the future is only that which has been interwoven with it in this

bygone time.   Yet it is for the individual
to bring into the superphysical world of
the future everything that he can draw
forth from the world of the senses.   If he
should only bring that which, coming from
the past, is commingled with his counter-
part, he would only partially have fulfilled
his earthly task.   Therefore, after some
time the Greater Guardian of the Threshold is joined to the lesser.   The meeting
with the second Guardian shall again be
described in narrative form.

When the individual has recognised all
those qualities from which he has to free
himself, his way is stopped by a sublime
and luminous form, whose beauty it is quite
impossible to describe in human language.
This meeting occurs when the organs of
thinking, feeling, and willing have so far
loosened themselves, even in their physical
connections, that the regulation of their
reciprocal relations is no longer managed

12

by themselves, but by the higher consciousness, which has now entirely separated itself from physical conditions. The organs of thought, feeling, and will have then become instruments in the power of the human soul, who exercises his controlling power over them from superphysical regions. The soul, thus liberated from all the bondage of sense, is now met by the second Guardian of the Threshold, who addresses him as follows :—

"You have freed yourself from the world of sense. You have won the right to settle in the superphysical world. From this you can now work. For your own part you no longer require your physical embodiment. If you should wish to acquire the faculties by which to dwell in this higher world, you no longer need to go back to the world of sense. Now gaze at me! Lo! how immeasurably sublime I stand, above all that you have at

present evolved out of yourself! You
have arrived at the present stage of your
progress towards perfection through the
faculties which you were able to develop in
the sense-world while you were still con-
fined to it. Now, however, must a period
begin in which your liberated powers may
act yet further upon the world of sense.
Hitherto you have but freed yourself, but
now can you go forth as a liberator of all
your fellows. As an individual have you
striven until to-day, but now shall you
associate yourself with the whole, so that
you may bring not yourself alone into the
superphysical world, but all things else
that exist in the world of phenomena. It
shall be open for you to unite yourself
with my form, but I cannot be blessed
where yet there is any one unredeemed!
As a separate freed-man you would like
to enter at once into the kingdom of the
superphysical, but then would you have

perforce to look down on the still unliber-
ated creatures in the world of sense, and
you would have separated your destiny
from theirs. Yet you and they are all
linked with each other. It is necessary
that all of you should descend into the
world of sense in order that you may
draw out of it the powers that are needed
for a higher world. If you should separate yourself from your fellows, you will
have misused the powers which you have
only been able to develop in common
with them. Had they not descended, the
descent had been impossible for you;
without them you had lacked the powers
that make up your superphysical existence. These powers for which you have
striven together with your fellows, you
must now in like manner share with them.
So long as you fail to apply every one of
your acquired powers to the liberation
of your companions, I shall obstruct your

entrance into the highest regions of the superphysical world. With those powers you have already won, you can stay in the lower regions of that world; but before the gates of the higher regions I stand as one of the cherubim with fiery sword in front of Paradise, to hinder your entrance as long as you have powers that remain unapplied to the world of sense. If you refuse to apply your powers in this way, others will come who will do so; and then will a lofty superphysical world receive all the fruits of the sense-world, but to you will be denied the very soil in which you were rooted. The world ennobled will develop itself beyond you, and you will be shut out therefrom. Then would your path be the black path, while those from whom you had severed yourself go forward on the white way."

So speaks the Greater Guardian of the Threshold soon after the meeting with the first watcher has taken place. The Initiate, however, knows exactly what lies before him if he should follow the allurements of a premature abode in the superphysical world. An indescribable splendour proceeds from the second Guardian of the Threshold; union with him appears as a remote ideal to the gazing soul, yet simultaneously comes the certitude that this union will only be possible if the Initiate has applied to the task of redeeming and liberating this world every power which has come to him therefrom. If he resolves to fulfil the demands of that luminous form, he becomes one of those who lead humanity to freedom. He brings his gifts to the altar of mankind. But if he prefers his own premature elevation into the super-physical world, then will he be submerged in the stream of human evolution. After his liberation from the world of sense he can win no new powers.   If he places his work at the disposal of the world, he must renounce the prospect of acquiring anything further for himself.

One cannot say that the individual would naturally choose the white path, when so called upon to make his decision. This depends entirely upon whether at the time of making the decision he is so exalted that no touch of selfishness would make the allurement of such beatitude appear desirable.   For these allurements are the strongest possible ; while, on the other side, no specific allurements exist. Nothing there evokes his egotism.   That which he obtains in the higher regions of the superphysical is nothing that comes *to* him, but solely something which proceeds *from* him—that is to say, the love of his fellows.   Nothing that egotism desires is denied upon the black path.   On the contrary, the fruits of this way consist precisely in the complete gratification of egotism, and therefore if any one merely desires bliss for himself, he would certainly travel down that way, since it is the appropriate path for him. No one, therefore, should expect the occultist of the white path to give him instruction concerning the development of his egotistical self. The occultist has not the smallest interest in the beatification of the individual. Each can attain that for himself. It is not the task of the white occultist to accelerate it. He is only concerned with the evolution and liberation of all those beings who are human or akin to the human. Therefore they give instructions only as to how one may use one's powers in co-operation with that work. Consequently, they place before all other attributes those of selfless devotion and self-sacrifice. They do not actually refuse any one, for even the most egotistical can ennoble themselves; but he who merely seeks something for himself, so long as he continues to do so will gain nothing from the occultist.   Indeed, even if the latter did not refuse him help, he would deprive himself of the natural effects of that assistance.   He who really follows out the instructions of the good occult teachers will understand the demands of the Greater Guardian after he has crossed the threshold; but he who does not follow these instructions cannot hope ever to reach the threshold.   Their instructions lead to the good, or else they are without effect at all; for to guide us to egotistical beatitude and a mere existence in the superphysical world is outside the circle of their task.   It is part of their duty to hold back the student from the celestial world until he can enter it with a will devoted entirely to selfless labour.

PRINTED BY NEILL AND CO., LTD., EDINBURGH.

Printed in the United States
1161200002B/11-12